BROKEN
umbrellas

BROKEN umbrellas

EMMA BROCH STUART

Unless otherwise indicated, all Scripture quotations are taken from the Holy Bible, New Living Translation, copyright © 1996, 2004, 2007, 2013 by Tyndale House Foundation. Used by permission of Tyndale House Publishers, Inc., Carol Stream, Illinois 60188. All rights reserved.

Scripture quotations marked (NIV) are taken from the Holy Bible, New International Version®, NIV®. Copyright © 1973, 1978, 1984, 2011 by Biblica, Inc.™ Used by permission of Zondervan. All rights reserved worldwide. www.zondervan.com The "NIV" and "New International Version" are trademarks registered in the United States Patent and Trademark Office by Biblica, Inc.™

Scriptures noted The Message are taken from THE MESSAGE. Copyright © by Eugene H. Peterson 1993, 1994, 1995, 1996, 2000, 2001, 2002. Used by permission of Tyndale House Publishers, Inc.

Scriptures noted NLV are taken from the New Life Version. Translators Ledyard, Gleason H. and Kathryn Ledyard. Copyright © 1969 by Christian Literature International (Canby, OR).

Scriptures noted NKJV are taken from the New King James Version®. Copyright © 1982 by Thomas Nelson. Used by permission. All rights reserved.

Scriptures noted NCV are taken from the New Century Version®. Copyright © 2005 by Thomas Nelson. Used by permission. All rights reserved.

Scriptures noted The Voice are taken from The Voice™. Copyright © 2008 by Ecclesia Bible Society. Used by permission. All rights reserved.

Scripture quotations marked ESV are from the ESV® Bible (The Holy Bible, English Standard Version®), copyright © 2001 by Crossway, a publishing ministry of Good News Publishers. Used by permission. All rights reserved.

BROKEN UMBRELLAS

Copyright © 2015, Emma Broch Stuart
All rights reserved. Reproduction in part or in whole is strictly forbidden without the express written consent of the publisher.

WhiteFire Publishing
13607 Bedford Rd NE
Cumberland, MD 21502

ISBN: 978-1-939023-48-3 (digital)
          978-1-939023-47-6 (print)

For broken people everywhere.

If your heart is broken, you'll find God right there.
~ Psalm 34:18 (The Message)

table of contents

Introduction...9
Chapter 1: Broken Umbrellas 13
Chapter 2: Until Death Do Us Part 17
Chapter 3: Widowed by Divorce................................21
Chapter 4: Inevitable Love...25
Chapter 5: Wobbling Towers......................................29
Chapter 6: Leaving a Legacy......................................33
Chapter 7: Between Edith and Evelyn.......................37
Chapter 8: *Hesed* Love...43
Chapter 9: Surrender..47
Chapter 10: A Pile of Dust...53
Chapter 11: Enough Is Enough..................................59
Chapter 12: That None Should Perish.......................63
Chapter 13: Ungodly Tornadoes.................................67
Chapter 14: Step Under..73
Chapter 15: Dangling Bitter Grapes...........................77
Chapter 16: Blame Game..83
Chapter 17: Rain Check...87
Chapter 18: Rope Holders..91
Chapter 19: Gloriously Equipped...............................95
Chapter 20: Neon Lights..103
Chapter 21: Cave of Fasting.....................................109
Chapter 22: Gently Broken.......................................113
Chapter 23: Stones of Abuse....................................119
Chapter 24: Pleasant Boundaries.............................125
Chapter 25: New Name...131
Chapter 26: Shamelessly Summarized.....................139
Chapter 27: Rabid Snares...145
Chapter 28: Wicked Dance.......................................159
Chapter 29: Elevator, Eyebrows, and Men of God...165
Chapter 30: Emotion or Verb...................................171

Chapter 31: Redeeming Fields...181
Chapter 32: Above All Else...189
Chapter 33: Knee to Knee..197
Chapter 34: Baby Wind..203
Chapter 35: Love Notes...207
Chapter 36: Joy Boxes...211
Chapter 37: Imperfect Skirts...219
Chapter 38: Go Knowing..227
Acknowledgments..231
References...233

introduction

BROKEN umbrellas

I take down a soup bowl from the cupboard, scratch off the dried bits the dishwasher failed to remove, and set it at my place. The second bowl I pull down makes me laugh. Dried glue still clings to the noticeable break line from where I expertly repaired my favorite bowl. The lime green one with MOM written on the side. Of course the O is now lopsided. I place the crooked bowl on the table and reach for another one.

Funny how I never noticed the brokenness when setting the table for just myself. I need new dishes.

I need a new life.

I give myself a shake. No. I will serve a meal with what I have and leave the rest up to God.

Steam escapes the pot, and I give the contents a quick stir. I sigh, imagining my readers' reaction to the meal I'm preparing for them. It's very fitting really. Soup in broken bowls, served by a broken hostess.

Emma Broch Stuart

Standing at the kitchen sink the other day, I wondered how to do the research for a book on brokenness since I'm not a schooled theologian. I suddenly realized I've *lived* the research, and that is theology. Theology, at its core, is simply knowing God. So then, a theologian is simply someone who believes anything about God.[1]

That by no means makes me an expert on brokenness, but with a past full of it, I have a genuine understanding of the subject. Beth Moore, in her book *So Long, Insecurity,* explains how God exposed every insecurity she had to make her a genuine writer on the subject.[2]

Broken Umbrellas is authentic. This I promise you. Brokenness consumed me and defined me most of my life. Even though I now stand in victory, I admit I'm not so eager to relive that brokenness through the pages of this book. Finding the courage to be vulnerable with you comes from God. If I relied on my own strength, *Broken Umbrellas* would not exist.

At times I prefer to shut the door on my past and forge ahead with all the knowledge and wisdom I've gleaned from God's healing. But God didn't bring me through this to keep the richness of His healing to myself. I must declare His glory. My testimony may help one person find their healing—or better yet, their Healer—and that one life is worth being vulnerable.

one

broken

umbrellas

BROKEN umbrellas

It snowed the day of my grandson's funeral. Pure grace blanketing dirty mounds of earth moved aside to make room for the baby life now gone. Softness floated down as we wept at the graveside. Through my tears, my gaze fell on a sagging blue umbrella suspended over the head of a woman grieving our tiny loss. Grieving with my family. New tears sprang from within me—from depths I didn't know existed. Not from the loss of my precious one, but from this old umbrella, broken and twisted, yet hovering and flapping above this woman. It offered no protection at all from the wetness dropping from the sky, yet she clung to it. Broken and unsheltered. Could anything symbolize my heart—and all humanity—better than this crippled umbrella? And then she did something that tore me apart. She moved her brokenness in an attempt to protect the man beside her.

Brokenness around us is easier to see than brokenness within ourselves. Just as the woman at my grandson's funeral tried to cover the man beside her with her broken umbrella, we relate and serve, love and protect with our brokenness. People still end up covered in life's bad weather. *We* still end up covered in snow. And we wonder why.

Hurts happen through relationships, but there is One Relationship that will heal the hurt. We have a relational God and He created us for relationship. Many of us don't realize our relationship umbrellas are broken.

We carry on attempting to cover those around us with our brokenness. Our friendships suffer. Family hurts spill over into generation after generation. We say marriage vows, but our brokenness will prevent us from keeping our promises to love and honor. Our intentions are honorable, but reality has proven time and time again that even honorable intentions have PMS, or get fired from work, or sit up all night with a sick baby, thus causing love and honor to fly out the window during spats and cranky arguments with the one we pledged so much to.

Why is it so hard to relate to others? It's not like trying to dry wet clothes in a blender. A blender blends. A dryer dries clothes. We were made for relationship, but all of us struggle with the one thing we were created for.

Broken relationships have been evident since the beginning. All we need are a few tents, some manna dropping from the sky, and we're the Israelites all over again.

There was a small sliver of time where all was right with relationships. I can imagine being there, surrounded by the splendor of a newly created world, where God walked with us in the cool of the day, conversed with us, delighted in us as we discovered. Pure. Just Him and us with the whole world at our feet.

Every once in a while, I glimpse that perfectness. It's like I stop being my broken self for a second and actually feel heaven's

BROKEN umbrellas

breeze upon my face. When that happens, there is absolutely nowhere for brokenness to cling to me. It's like when Peter stepped out of the boat and walked toward Jesus in Matthew 14:29. In those few moments, he was not a broken human being living in a broken world. He glimpsed and grasped wholeness.

Only Christ's wholeness will heal our brokenness. And it's a journey.

Here's a glimpse at mine.

two until death do us part

BROKEN umbrellas

A precious friend going through a divorce has chosen a black dress to wear to court. The symbolism didn't strike her until she hung it in the very closet—in the very place—her wedding dress hung thirteen years earlier. The purity of blissful life circled around to the anguish of death—and I grieve with her. As God turns her ashes to beauty, a new dress will soon hang in that closet. A dress of joy, grace, and new beginnings.

My first husband, Dan, was a transvestite.

Unimaginable brokenness was brought front and center in my marriage on a daily basis. I died many times during this relationship—each and every time I witnessed or experienced something God never intended for marriage. Death was inevitable. Death *did* part us, and yet our physical hearts never stopped beating.

Each of us endures many deaths during our life here on earth. Circumstances change, seasons of life occur, relationships end, and all the while our hearts keep beating.

Death is the "destruction or termination of anything." And when death happens to a marriage, divorce becomes its funeral.

Very few healthy pieces of me existed after the funeral. But I carried those pieces—plus all the broken, twisted pieces I picked up during the marriage—and walked into another intimate relationship. You see, my first marriage twenty-seven years ago began what can only be described as a "collection" of broken relationships.

Most agree my divorce from Dan was justified, based solely on what the word *transvestite* implies and what society accepts as a valid reason for divorce. This dysfunctional element in the marriage caused trust to die, along with intimacy, self-worth, and respect. But I have experienced deaths of these same things in other relationships and transvestism wasn't the killer. More times than not, selfishness or pride caused these deaths. Spiritual death or physical death, something was destroyed, terminated.

Our *broken* society takes broken marriages on an individual basis and judges which ones rightfully ended in divorce and which ones didn't. Most of us agree that when abuse is the cause of a broken marriage, divorce is justified. Same with infidelity. But if we embraced individuals and left the judging to God, a lot more people would seek healing instead of shriveling up in isolation and depression, wishing they would physically die.

I'm so passionate about this subject because I've been deeply

BROKEN umbrellas

hurt by so many people—and I've been deeply healed by the only One who matters. Please hear my heart. I'm not an advocate for divorce. I'm an advocate for broken people, and people suffering the effects of divorce make up a large percentage of the population. We can't ignore this.

Divorced people mourn—and they mourn deep. Marital deaths hurt—and they hurt deep. By the time divorce seems like the only option, most people have suffered horrendous marital deaths that affect the very core of their being. And we hurt them—and God—when we try to shove them aside.

We have enough people telling us divorce is wrong, that divorce is the biggest sin. We don't have enough people who say, "Divorce happens because we live in a broken world. I'm here for you, how can I help?" We do people a terrible injustice when we aren't willing—or able—to enter their stories. Grasp. Walk in their shoes if only through listening. Who among us will boldly go into the pit of hell—*death*—and sit with a person whose heart carries such burdens?

three

widowed

by

divorce

BROKEN umbrellas

Hidden passageways lurk around every dark corner of that pit. I cling to the tiniest hope, a sliver of joy, or strand of frayed rope. Maybe tomorrow the stranger in my husband's shoes will disappear and the one I pledged to honor and love will return. He doesn't, and I mourn his death.

I married Ed fourteen years ago, and it lasted ten years before I found myself divorced again. But it was the first time I allowed myself to mourn and did not hurry to the next broken relationship. Widowhood was a new status for me. Or was it? Maybe I only see it now because God orchestrated a period of mourning.

That divorce—funeral—is my point of reference when I look for spiritual growth within myself. Every seminar I've attended during the past four years, along with every conference, workshop, Bible study, or "get to know each other" conversation refers me back to this life-altering event. And it precedes the most amazing healing celebration. But more on that in later chapters.

Right now, I want to sit with you. Enter your pit. Grasp. Walk in your shoes, if only through sharing my own story. And we'll start here, with my marriage to Ed.

So, how does one come to the realization that their spouse has been replaced by a complete stranger? It's not like aliens abducted your true love in the night and you realize it first thing the next morning. It's definitely not as obvious as switching on or off a light. The process is slow, extremely painful…and accepting that your spouse is never coming back can be depressing and frightening, but also the first step to mourning.

Even though I endured much pain at the hands of others prior to this latest alien abduction (sometimes I wondered), I want to settle here, on this relationship, because it is pivotal to my healing—which is the point of this book.

This broken relationship is also more relevant because I was a Christian—as was he. Before that, I lived by a different standard.

I found Christ during my marriage to Ed and fell under the

BROKEN umbrellas

false assumption that doing so would heal the brokenness in my relationship. Finding Christ meant that the stranger would soon go away, and the person I married would reappear and be better than ever because he found Christ at the same time I did. We even celebrated this by being baptized together before our Christian brothers and sisters.

Little did I know, the brokenness could—and did—get a lot worse. Marital deaths suffered up to this point were only the beginning. This stranger occupying my husband's body became the enemy, someone to fear. Not an obvious fear like I felt when physically abused in the past. No, this fear was darker, more oppressive. Satan was after my soul.

four

inevitable

love

BROKEN umbrellas

Wrinkles, uncovered and smiling
Morning coffee in the perfect cup
Ink
Raindrops clinging to winter branches
Trees caught between seasons
Raspberries
Tea parties
Pangs of hunger and a full cupboard
Lush ivy swaying in the breeze
Eyebrows
Starting over with each sunrise

~ excerpt from my gratitude journal

Broken things fascinate me. How did they break? Can they be repaired? If so, are they ever the same again?

Many treasures can be found at second-hand shops. I'm drawn to objects that have endured major wear and tear, only to be left dented and scarred. Sometimes as I inflict wear and tear on things around the house, I stop and imagine that skillet or book sitting in a second-hand shop. Would anyone notice the scratches or bent pages and wonder how they got there? If they closed their eyes, could they see me scrubbing burnt egg off the skillet?

My daughter inherited this love of recycled treasures. Recently, she found a LOVE shirt with the attributes of love written all over it. Tiny metal chains—with links broken in several places—ran across the front of it. The thing was a rag. Really. But she *needed* it so badly that I bought it for her, confident I could fix the broken spots.

She wears it all the time. It's one of those tops we'll see in every photo until she grows out of it, and then she'll want to save it for her daughter. (We have a closet full of those treasures.)

I found it ironic that the little chains broke in many places on a shirt with LOVE splattered across it.

One of the characteristics of love inked across my daughter's favorite shirt is *inevitable*. Thinking back fourteen years ago, I would agree that love was inevitable—"unavoidable, regardless of the circumstances; certain to occur."

Ed and I overcame many obstacles, including different continents, to be together. This inevitable love started out the classic way: sweet, attentive, gracious. I won't take the time to fill in the basics. It started strong enough, and you know it ended with me being widowed—divorced.

While this inevitable human love did eventually end in death on many levels, God's inevitable love was and is stable, *unfailing*, dependable, and never ends. I cling to the safety of knowing God is unchanging, therefore a stranger can never occupy His

BROKEN umbrellas

shoes. I will never wake up one morning and wonder if aliens abducted the One who husbands me right now. Spine-shivering fear evaporates when I rest in the shelter of His wing. I follow as He leads me through the valley of the shadow of death. After all, it's only a shadow.

If God knows where the best pastures are, surely He knows the best path for me—even if it leads through valleys. Growth is inevitable when walking in the valley among lush fruits and trickling brooks. Vegetation thrives in the valley. Why would I be any different?

I stroll along calm waters, stronger in my faith, despite the brokenness I have endured. God uses it all for His glory. His inevitable glory.

five wobbling towers

BROKEN umbrellas

We only think we've matured beyond using toy blocks to build our towers. Nowhere is it more evident than on the playground of our lives that we still compete to see who can build the tallest tower.

Chapters like the previous one refresh me and give me strength to keep telling my story. I need those reminders that there are calm waters on the other side of this hard stuff we're talking about. And it's about to get harder. I know what you're thinking. How can anything be harder than being married to a transvestite? Harder than physical abuse? Harder than years and years of lugging my brokenness from one intimate relationship to another, all the while adding to the brokenness, the burden growing heavier and heavier?

Matthew 1:25 says, "And Joseph named him Jesus." Jesus had a Father—and a direct line to Him—but He also had an earthly dad. Joseph is by far one of my favorite people in the Bible. The impact Joseph had on Jesus's life is so precious to me. Joseph made the decision to love and care for the Savior. I love that Joseph taught carpentry to the Carpenter of the universe.

Fourteen years ago, when I crossed the Atlantic Ocean, I didn't cross it alone. My two sons made the voyage with me. Ed made the decision to love and care for them and welcomed all three of us with open arms. Of course, I dragged all my former relationship baggage across the Atlantic.

I think we subconsciously go into a relationship thinking it will miraculously heal all the hurt from past relationships. It doesn't. And we end up with this wobbling tower of brokenness. Before we know it, the elephant in the room knocks over our wobbling tower and our brokenness shatters like a crystal vase.

It's so discouraging. I mean, do people have any idea how much glue we use to put our broken pieces back together so we *appear* to be healthy, thriving adults? Appearances seem to be all that matter.

The most broken thing we do is strive for outward perfection

BROKEN umbrellas

and live our lives as if we don't need the Glue that fixes everything. Not that pathetic glue we use to patch up our broken appearances, or our favorite lime-green bowl. Christ and Christ alone is the Glue that can heal deep-rooted brokenness (Luke 4:18).

Like I said, the relationship started out sweet, attentive, and gracious. After three years of marriage, in vitro fertilization gave us a beautiful daughter. Ed changed jobs for something closer to home, taking a significant cut in salary, and threatened to divorce me if I didn't find work—his answer to our money problems. He refused to ask for his previous job back—my answer to our money problems. Part-time cleaning jobs for minimum wage were all I had found the first three years. Nothing on my resume was valid in France. In order to find a well-paying job, I would have to go to school again—*in French!* This was not an option for two reasons: first, my French was not good enough; and second, we couldn't afford to pay for school. I found a part-time job, but we still were not making ends meet.

The tower was wobbling, but the elephant hadn't knocked it over yet.

Disrespect on both sides wiggled in. Bickering, nagging, and periods of silence clouded the relationship. The elephant in the room—napping at this point—began to stir. For years I lulled him back to sleep by patting his back with one hand, while using the other hand to keep my wobbling tower standing. Ed and I would meet up in the bedroom after a day of disrespect and bickering, and sex patched things up (sleep, elephant, sleep).

Six and a half years into the marriage, that elephant woke up, and my wobbling tower of brokenness started crashing.

six

leaving a legacy

BROKEN umbrellas

Humpty Dumpty sat on a wall, Humpty Dumpty had a great fall. All the king's horses and all the king's men couldn't put Humpty together again.

Ed and I did not make a strong marital team. When one of my children showed signs of dire distress, we did not join forces in order to strengthen our family and overcome this crisis. Ed withdrew, leaving me to face it alone. I increased the nagging. That stupid elephant. My family was hurting, and appearances no longer mattered. I grasped at any hope, any help.

In the midst of disaster, someone—I don't even remember who—invited me to a women's inspirational breakfast. The speaker spoke on "Leaving a Legacy." It made me roll my eyes with sarcasm. The only legacy I was leaving my children was how to lull an elephant to sleep—and not even doing a good job of that at the moment.

Apparently, I wore my withering heart on my sleeve because the woman sitting beside me asked just the right questions. Before I knew it, I was sobbing. She cried with me, and we sat in our tears long after the breakfast ended. She and her husband took Ed and me under their wing, counseling us for months and going through a Bible study on finding Christ.

I clung to that. Would Jesus fix my marriage? My child? Me? I gave my life to Christ six months after attending that women's breakfast. Ed also came to Christ. We did it together. Nothing could harm our marriage now. My child was also getting help. We were on the right path as a family.

I sincerely believed I would never see that elephant again.

seven

between

edith

and

evelyn

BROKEN umbrellas

Pain isn't always a bad thing. It lets us know when something is wrong, broken, or needs Jesus.

I know the previous chapter is a short one. I just don't feel led to add any more to it. I sense a change in the rhythm of my writing as we delve into the murky waters still fresh in my mind and heart. Bear with me. Oh, how I desperately want to get to the rejoicing part of this book! But I also don't want to rush this painful part. It makes the healing so much more victorious.

So, I succeeded in gluing my tower of broken pieces back together. How could I have ever anticipated that in a matter of months, a whole herd of elephants would come stomping through my life?

My oldest son was arrested for theft. The child in dire distress took a turn for the worse and drastic measures needed to be taken. My other child was victimized. And beyond all that, Ed became the enemy.

I was assaulted on all fronts. I questioned God's trustworthiness. I was stabbing elephants left and right, screaming out to God. I was so lost, so confused. I didn't understand why I was going through so many trials. I'd just found Christ, finally understood what it meant to be in a relationship with Him. Why this? Why now? The battle was intense. I clung to God for every breath, and then yelled at Him because it hurt so much. Never had I been overcome with such helplessness and suffering.

The desperation of my life had never been so heavy. I lived ten lifetimes of experiences without Christ and never suffered like this. I swore God worked on an alphabetical system where people rode a conveyor belt and the funnel was stuck between Edith and Evelyn—over me, Emma—and I was receiving all of Evelyn's trials. Talk about wanting to find a crowbar and get that assembly line moving! I just couldn't carry any more.

My life greatly resembled that of Job in the Bible when a series of calamities fell on him all at the same time (Job 1:13-19). Verses 14 says a messenger arrived at Job's home with news (bad

BROKEN umbrellas

news, of course). Verses 16 says that before the first messenger finished speaking, another messenger arrived with news. Verse 17 says that before the second messenger finished speaking, another messenger arrived with news. Then verse 18 says that before the third messenger finished speaking, a fourth messenger arrived with news. Four messengers arrived simultaneously with accounts of loss and despair. His oxen and donkeys were stolen; his farmhands were killed; his sheep and shepherds burned with the "fire of God"; raiders stole his camels and killed Job's servants; and a powerful wind killed his ten children.

And, "In all of this, Job did not sin by blaming God" (Job 1:22).

You already know that my marriage didn't survive these trials. I hesitate here to share specific details of what I call "the end times." The last thing I want you to do is compare your marital deaths with mine. God is bigger than any situation we find ourselves in. He can redeem and heal any brokenness we have suffered—as well as caused.

Please know that I am not suggesting you divorce your spouse, but that you go to the Lord with your hurts and brokenness. He *is* trustworthy. I trust Him now to show me how much to share. It's important that you grasp just how deep my pit was.

Ed's sins seemed to have no limits—despite accepting Christ or being dunked in the same baptismal waters as I. I often wondered if his conversion was sincere. That is between him and God. I do know that when one walks with Christ, fruit of that relationship is visible. I did not see any with Ed, and his sins grew heavier as time went by.

One example was with our neighbor. She was quite eccentric and often vulgar. She prayed to her dead grandma, dabbled in all religions, and wore a seahorse skeleton around her neck for protection. Ed loved when she and her husband invited us over. He would dash out the door, often leaving me to pray alone as I lagged behind. I prayed for spiritual protection and that we would be an example of Christ to this lost family. I sat and listened to this neighbor's sexual innuendos toward Ed, her husband laughing along with them. I intercepted topless vacation photos before they could be passed to Ed, all the while a scowl darkening his face as he glared at me. Of course I subjected myself to these visits because I couldn't let my husband go alone. Of course I nagged about ungodly behavior when we returned home. Of course it changed nothing.

To add to the chaos—because let's face it, the funnel of that conveyor belt is still stuck between Edith and Evelyn, over me—I was injured at work, forcing me to take disability, and Ed lost his job. I can't even type that sentence without crying. I remember those dark days like they were yesterday. Don't get me wrong, I want to remember. Always. But that doesn't mean it's easy. I never want to forget, because that makes living in the light so much sweeter.

Never have I felt more alone than those last two years of the marriage when Ed was unemployed. I'm home nursing an injury to my arm; he's home succumbing to the woes of losing his job. Marital deaths breed. Multiply. Dead elephants litter our lives; new elephants appear to crush any attempt at gluing the tower of brokenness.

eight

hesed

love

BROKEN umbrellas

Waves of love crash along the shores of our hearts. Our children leave treasures from the sea for us to gather and hold precious. Sweet memories. And painful ones. We count their toes, hold their hands, and cry when they fall. Not every seashell-treasure arrives on the shore intact. Some are broken, weathered, or smashed to smithereens. But the sands of love need each and every one to create hearts that endure the elements of life.

Let's pause here and talk about one very significant lesson God taught me during this dark period. It's a lesson I wasn't even aware I was learning.

Our ultimate job as parents is to prepare our children for the real world and teach them to navigate that world independently. Our training and wisdom can only go so far. We as parents must resist carrying our children's sin on our shoulders. When we try to carry it, it makes the situation about us, not about them or the lessons God can teach them in their darkest days.

My oldest son's arrest broke this mama's heart. To watch the police fingerprint him before turning him over to my custody literally twisted my guts. If he hadn't been an adult—barely—I would have put him over my knee right there in front of the cops. After spanking the daylights out of my son, I would have held him in my arms and begged the officer to fingerprint me instead. I would have taken his sin on my shoulders to spare him this life lesson.

As parents, we can fall into a trap of making our children's mistakes our mistakes. We take it personally when they mess up, like our good mama name has been stained. Their bad decisions put our parenting into question. We somehow failed in bringing them up.

It's broken and twisted to take our children's sin upon ourselves because it means we believe free will applies to everyone…except our offspring. Jesus died for everyone's sin…except the sin of our child—that reflects on us somehow.

Honestly, this is how I would have reacted and believed. Only, there was no room on my shoulders to carry my son's sin, even if I wanted to. I was so burdened by everything else—Ed alone weighed a ton—there simply was not room to carry this and turn it into being about me as a mother.

Because I could not carry my son's sin, I did the only thing I could do. I gave him unconditional love, remained by his side, and encouraged him that this was an awesome lesson to learn.

BROKEN umbrellas

I praised him for facing the consequences and prayed over him, despite his unbelief in God.

And the results were immediate. He went from a disposition of stone during the arrest, interrogation, and fingerprinting, to melted butter when I got him out of that station and immediately loved on him.

It was at that moment I grasped *hesed* love—faithful, loyal love. I glimpsed how it could be possible for God to love us in spite of our sin nature.

Carolyn Custis James, in her book *The Gospel of Ruth*, describes *hesed* as selfless love rooted in commitment, not obligation. She explains that *hesed* love inspires someone—me as a mother—to go above and beyond what is expected.[3]

People are watching. They observe. This is by far the biggest ministry God calls us to, more than hands-on, more than head knowledge. Example. How we as Christians deal with a crisis, how we love when we don't think anyone else is watching. How we live out our Christian walk. It's all being observed.

Little did I know that my *expression* of unconditional love showed my son's girlfriend the *meaning* of unconditional love. I am so thankful that God prompted my heart and gave me the words to say during a conversation with her. She and my son hadn't been dating long when he was arrested. She went with me to the police station. She asked me how I could be so calm when she was furious. Oh, I was furious, and I told her so. I also sensed that love was conditional for her. That my son had messed up big time and she no longer "loved" him. God guided that conversation, and when she got out of the car, she also embraced my son with unconditional love.

nine
surrender

BROKEN umbrellas

Do you ever have a spurt of growth where you feel a little heaviness lift and are able to breathe a little deeper—like a baby bean sprout poking through the earth? And then someone comes along and plucks your one and only, itty bitty leaf, not even giving you a chance to unfurl and reach toward the sun so you can blossom and produce your fruit. Just when you gain a little strength, start sprouting again, that same person plucks your brand new leaf. It's like your tiny spurts of growth feed them, and you are left withering time and time again.

Actually giving *hesed* and grasping the concept both encouraged me and depressed me. I committed to discipling my son's girlfriend and teaching her about Christ. At the same time, I realized that *hesed* worked in marriages too, and surrendered to the belief that God expected me to remain in this broken relationship. I obeyed, but I also grieved.

Nagging took on a whole new level. I had nothing to lose at this point. Ed neglected; I nagged. Ed watched porn; I nagged. Ed lied; I nagged. Ed lusted; I nagged. It broke me so much just to go to the store with him. When I did, I made sure to go through a checkout with an older woman or man. I couldn't bear Ed flirting with women—in my presence. I couldn't bear the ogling.

But most of all, I couldn't bear sitting beside him in church, supporting him by my mere presence. Supporting his sin, his lust of my precious sisters in Christ. I tried to protect them, to nudge him, to stand between them if he engaged them in conversation. I blocked his view when he leaned back in his seat. Made excuses for him, or cleared my throat to divert his attention. I begged him to stop, to get help. He denied having a problem.

Remembering this pain empties me. I'm sobbing as I relive it for you on these pages, yet I need to sit in that for a minute and feel it again. Feel the death—those parts of me that broke beyond repair, because I want you to grasp this. The grief was so hard to bear. To sit, sobbing, beside this man in church as he lusted. Every Sunday was like a funeral, where I laid another piece of me to rest. Forever.

Aware that in God's eyes, lust is the same as adultery (Matthew 5:28), I couldn't go on like this. I sought help and enrolled us in a Christian marriage seminar. I may have surrendered and accepted this as my lot in life, but my heart was desperate for anything that could salvage our marriage—or make it more tolerable.

BROKEN umbrellas

At the seminar, I watched other husbands with a desire to glean wisdom for the betterment of their relationship. As I observed their sincere hearts, bitterness grew in mine, and jealousy that my husband was the only one leering at female backsides or staring at cleavage. At a week-long workshop for *marriage*, no less.

And I buried another piece of me.

Little by little, I lowered my expectations of Ed as well as the relationship in order to make the disappointment more bearable. The less I expected, the easier it was to accept nothing.

I stopped inviting friends over. How could I subject them to that hovering cloud of darkness? Evil had invaded my home. My marriage.

The weight of Ed settled on my shoulders like a dead corpse. I carried him everywhere, dragged him at times.

Ed continued to "talk the Christian talk"—which disgusted me. It twisted my guts. I focused on my son's girlfriend—a distraction, which in and of itself was a good thing. To pour your energy into someone besides yourself is honorable.

I found a Bible study that covered the basics in simple terminology and walked with my son's girlfriend through this Bible study, praying she would discover Christ. All the while, I deceived myself into thinking Ed and I were showing her Christ, that we'd put ourselves aside and our example was shining through. That by somehow focusing on someone else—someone lost—we as a couple could be saved.

The day I discovered Ed was touching her inappropriately—and had been doing so for more than a year—I completely lost it. I only thought I had reached the bottom of that pit. She was like a daughter to us. To Ed. It sickened me. How could this have escaped my attention? How could I have been so careful to "protect" my sisters in Christ that I failed this precious young woman?

Welcome to Christianity!

Emma Broch Stuart

Bitter. I was so bitter. Now Ed couldn't even pass me in the hallway without me nagging uncontrollably. Anger and bitterness consumed me, made me ugly.

But I continued to carry Ed—and his sins.

ten

a pile
of
dust

BROKEN umbrellas

My friends rescued a dog that had been chained up and left to starve. They allowed the dog to be inside, but he had to stay on his mat. Many times, he snuck over to me and rested his head in the crook of my elbow. His eyes spoke volumes about his life, and I related to his old wounds of suffering. I myself have been chained up and left to starve. Only difference is the person who chained and starved me—Ed—stood within sight, but was unreachable. He stood there, mocking me with neglect and emotional starvation. Clearly able to give nourishment, he chose not to. I guess this dog was lucky; he didn't see the person starving him—a constant reminder that food was available, but that the person chose not to feed him.

Until now, I've only skimmed the surface of the neglect I suffered in those end times. We're closing in on the "funeral." *We're nearly there*, as my British friend would say.

For the funeral, I actually made a list of all the relationship hurts—marital deaths. Of course, the list was just for my own private ceremony, alone and sobbing. Human beings need things to make sense. And nothing made sense. Believe it or not, the most senseless thing about it all was how long I hung on.

Neglect, deliberate and excruciating, is at the top of the list for the most horrendous abuses. Indescribable deaths occur within a person's soul. Their very core suffers over and over.

After a day of complete rejection and isolation, Ed would suddenly come alive and be charming to me—when someone was watching. Ed neglected me in private and mocked me in public by reaching for my hand to show the world that he was an attentive husband. It's safe to assume I withdrew from his touch, angry that he would put on such a show. This, of course, only proved one thing to the world: I was the problem.

Reading *The Five Love Languages* by Gary Chapman helped me discover that my love language is quality time.[4] Ed refused to speak my language. Not out of ignorance, but out of deliberate disdain for me and our marriage. Showing me affection in public only proved he was capable of giving attention. Ed's love language was physical touch.[5] By this point, I'd fallen into a cycle of speaking his love language in hope of improving the marriage; and not speaking his love language in hope that it would wake him up. Both only increased the lust and porn.

Over the course of the end times, I found any excuse to leave the house—and the evil that lurked there—a couple times a week. God surrounded me with women who lifted me up in prayer. Weekly Bible studies gave me courage. Yearly women's retreats gave me strength. I grew in my faith despite the difficulties. But,

BROKEN umbrellas

I found it increasingly hard to "lead a double life." I honored God while out with friends, doing Bible studies or participating in ministry. However, my heart would turn to stone the rest of the time. Enduring Ed's neglect brought uncountable tears on uncountable occasions.

Ed stopped wanting intimacy but started molesting me in my sleep. I grew so afraid. My health suffered. My woman's heart lay in tatters. I begged God for mercy and cried out for reprieve.

Because I still believed it was God's will for me to endure this suffering, I continued to reach out to anyone willing to lend a hand. Ed and I were counseled by our pastor and the leader of our small group on basic marital conflicts. (I still carried the weight of Ed's sins and didn't expose the more severe ones.) I was advised repeatedly to stay in the marriage. Stay at all costs. Increase intimacy. Forgive. Submit. Stay.

If Ed did become interested in intimacy—while I was awake, that is—I started insisting that he pray over our marriage first, as well as pray over our sex life. For a few months, I deceived myself into thinking we were going to be okay. For goodness sake, we were praying together before sex. There's nothing more intimate than an intimate conversation with God before engaging in intimacy.

Nothing had changed otherwise. Ed continued to neglect me—continued to sin with lust—and I continued to sin with nagging. We met up occasionally for intimacy—oh, and prayer. I told myself to give it time. That it would all work out in the end. I continued seeking strength from outside sources (godly friends, Bible study/prayer, workshops on marriage, books).

I ignored the newest warning signs Ed was emanating: aggressiveness in bed; browsing for women on dating sites; and if possible, even more neglect. I counted the words he spoke to me in a given day. I woke up one morning and told myself I was going to count how many words came out of his mouth that were directed at me. Five. Home with him from sun up to sun down and he spoke five words to me. One sentence. *Do you have any money?*

And then the elephant of all elephants stood and crushed my tower of brokenness to a pile of dust. Ed admitted he didn't love me. He admitted that any acts of intimacy he had engaged in were not those of a husband to his wife. He was treating me like a prostitute. I gave Ed an ultimatum to either change or get a divorce. He said he didn't want to change; he would rather divorce, but he wanted to wait three months in order to make the transition easier.

Forget the glue to try and salvage the shards of our broken marriage. The only thing I could do with this was grab a dust pan and a broom.

> *Do not let any part of your body become an instrument of evil to serve sin. Instead, give yourselves completely to God, for you were dead, but now you have new life. So use your whole body as an instrument to do what is right for the glory of God* (Romans 6:13).

eleven

enough

is

enough

BROKEN umbrellas

The Lord helps them and takes them out of trouble. ***He takes them away from the sinful,*** *and saves them, because they go to Him for a safe place* (Psalm 37:40 NLV, emphasis added).

I volunteered at a church camp that final summer before the funeral—right after the ultimatum—and took my daughter with me. Ed stayed at home. I hadn't fully embraced his preference to divorce rather than change; he was probably blowing off steam. A lot could happen in three months.

Sitting in our living quarters at the camp, my daughter looked over at me and said, "We are so good here together, just you and me." I looked into the face of that little woman in training and my heart fell ten stories. What was I teaching her about marriage? She would learn—by my example—how to be a wife. I found a quiet place and poured my heart out to God.

I had already submitted to all the suffering Ed caused me, and resolved myself to the hand I had been dealt. But the thought of my daughter settling down with a man like her father tore me to shreds. That could be her path. I was showing her how to do it. How to carry a dead husband on her shoulders, how to enable him to sin and cover for it. How to buckle under abuse. How to nag because you can't stand the silence. Can't stand the neglect.

I begged God's forgiveness for the disobedience I assumed I was about to commit. For what I realized I had already done in my heart. Divorce my husband. And I wasn't waiting three months.

God immediately branded the words, "Enough is enough!" on my war-stricken, ragged heart. Then He swooped in and delivered me.

In some ways, this next phase was harder than the marital deaths I endured. I feared the unknown. I knew neglect like the back of my hand. Emotional abuse was my next of kin, but I wasn't familiar with this kind of deliverance—had never experienced it in all my life. It was amazingly peaceful and comforting and beautiful, yet frightening at the same time because something was now missing. Mind you, a negative, dark

BROKEN umbrellas

oppressiveness, but missing nonetheless. How was I supposed to fill that void? Being yoked for so many years to a person like Ed created some habits and mindsets that weren't easily shaken. I struggled to accept that the road to complete healing was long, the process painful and not instantaneous.

Suddenly on my own, I floated in a state of bewilderment for quite a while. The first time I woke up and wasn't in a muscle-tensed fetal position, it scared me. I just knew I must have let my guard down and ended up being molested in my sleep again. But I hadn't been, and I cried that my mind even went there.

I wasn't accustomed to the feel of empty shoulders. I hadn't even fully realized I was carrying Ed's dead corpse all those years—the weight had settled on me slowly over time. And I learned another valuable lesson. Just like a parent can't carry the sins of their children, a person can't carry the sins of their spouse.

twelve

that

none

should

perish

BROKEN umbrellas

[The Lord] is patient with you, not wanting anyone to perish, but everyone to come to repentance (2 Peter 3:9 NIV).

I sat for two days staring at the end of the previous chapter. What else can I say after such a profound realization? It left me—and still leaves me—breathless. I need to repeat the last line of the last chapter, more for myself than for you. *A person cannot carry the sins of their spouse.* They can try. I tried.

Let's be very clear here. When I say that a person cannot carry the sins of their spouse, I am talking about enabling a spouse to continue in sin, like I did by lowering my expectations to accommodate for Ed's sins. I am *not* talking about a spouse who confesses to struggling with something and together the couple faces that struggle, knowing the other may fall at times.

God sees our hearts. I truly believe this is the key to why He delivered me while perhaps telling someone else to stay. I had a conversation with a precious sister in Christ about this very thing. I shared with her that I clearly heard God impressing upon my heart, "Enough is enough." She found that interesting and said she too had gone to the Lord concerning some marital difficulties (different from mine, but damaging nonetheless) and God clearly said, "Stay."

God knows what it will take to bring someone to his or her knees in humble repentance. He knows what it will take to turn the heart of a person drowning in sin, and that very well may be the perseverance of a godly spouse.

I said earlier that the next phase was perhaps harder than enduring painful marital deaths. We can't skip over that phase. It's a pit of despair all by itself, so let's move on to the next chapter. But before we go to the dark corners of that pit, let me say something concerning Ed's heart. God deeply loves Ed and wants to draw him closer to His healing arms. It took a long time before I could sincerely pray for Ed. Before, while the pain was so raw, a precious friend offered to lift him up in prayer on my behalf. There aren't enough words to express how much that blessed me. God wants us to pray for one another—including

BROKEN umbrellas

hurtful spouses. I just couldn't pray for him at the time without turning it into a pity party for myself.

Would it be out of line to ask each of you to pray for Ed? To my knowledge, he is still in a difficult place in his life, and God doesn't want anyone to perish.

Let's pray together:

> *Father,*
>
> *We bring Ed before the throne and ask that You draw him closer to Your embrace. Surround him with godly people who invest in his life. Heal his spirit, his heart, his soul, his mind. Lord, do whatever it takes to bring him to his knees before You in humble repentance and sincere reverence. Your Word says that You don't want anyone to perish. We claim that for Ed right now, in the name of Your Son, Jesus Christ.*
> *Amen.*

thirteen

ungodly

tornadoes

BROKEN umbrellas

*"Don't pick on people, jump on their failures, criticize their faults—unless, of course, you want the same treatment. That critical spirit has a way of boomeranging. It's easy to see a smudge on your neighbor's face and be oblivious to the ugly sneer on your own. Do you have the nerve to say, 'Let me wash your face for you,' when your own face is distorted by contempt? It's this whole traveling road-show mentality all over again, **playing a holier-than-thou part instead of just living your part.** Wipe that ugly sneer off your own face, and you might be fit to offer a washcloth to your neighbor"* (Matthew 7:1-5 The Message, emphasis added).

It is indeed an amazing day when I would rather stay in the previous chapter and pray for Ed—oh, God is good! So, so good!—than start talking about the next pit, because now we are going to really churn up those murky waters.

It's hard to believe anything could damage and scar a heart already pulverized beyond human repair. But just as painful as the end times—more painful than the funeral—were the many occasions when Christians condemned me...in the name of the Lord.

The first inkling I had that leaving Ed wouldn't go over well with my church was while I was still serving at the church camp that last summer before the funeral. A sister in Christ stopped by the camp for the day and found me cleaning toilets in the dormitory. I confided in her that Ed and I had reached the end (she knew our marriage was suffering), and I would be moving out when I returned home from the camp. She asked, "Oh, did he abuse you?"

Imagine God on His hands and knees, already at work on that pile of dust called my life. He's sifting, making piles, preparing to rebuild my tower. This sister's condescending question blew right through like a tornado, scattering those piles.

My second clue was when I reached out to my pastor, asking him for help finding housing. His response was, "Don't leave [the marriage home] too quickly because there is no violence involved." He felt my decision was a hasty one. Even though he had mediated counseling and knew we were struggling. I informed him I would not be staying and would seek help elsewhere.

God immediately opened doors for housing, and I found myself nestled in a little town on the outskirts of a large city with public transportation and access to everything I needed—including an international church where I was accepted and loved unconditionally.

BROKEN umbrellas

Just because you leave *a* church, doesn't mean you leave *the* Church. All the evangelical churches in the area were connected through ministries, outreach, and activities. My fragile heart crossed paths on many occasions with brothers and sisters from my previous church. For a long time, their tornado-blowing winds tried to demolish the work God was doing in my life.

My heart still aches over the snubbing I received one day from three couples who were eating at a fast-food restaurant the same time I was. They seemed to walk right through me, with their eyes averted in order to avoid speaking to me. Could God's people act any more ungodly? Suddenly, I was the woman at the well, beneath them, not worthy to even be greeted as a fellow human being, let alone their sister in Christ struggling at the present moment. I don't know their hearts, but given my fragile state, I took this as a direct offense.

I'd like to believe they feared the reality I represented. Unfortunately, statistics show that these people will be touched by divorce. Would they be as condemning if it hit closer to home? A friend, family member, their sons or daughters? They themselves? Or would they excuse it—that whole pick-and-choose mentality our broken society has fallen into? It appeared their avoidance of me was condemnation, plain and simple, though there is nothing plain or simple about condemnation.

Another time at a community function, a man from my previous church asked me if I was Ed's ex-wife. I told him I was. He said, "Yeah, I remember you. God doesn't like divorce." I told him God also disapproved of judging. Then I excused myself to cry in the bathroom.

While there are many more incidents, these are enough examples to show the brokenness of God's people and how their sharp edges can cut deep into the hearts of those already hurting.

If I wasn't clinging to God before, I definitely clung to Him through these tornadoes. That pit was deep and so very painful. I still don't understand why abuse from Christians was more painful at times than other abuses I'd suffered. Maybe because I was already hurting so much, and my guard was down when relating with people who should possess the same qualities as Christ. I trusted that Christians who had walked with the Lord longer than I had surely knew more than I did, and that put me in an awful position. I was tempted at times to doubt God's voice that "enough is enough." I was so torn and really struggled—God delivered me, but the message I received from others was that a true Christian would have stayed in the marriage.

Satan was after my soul, and he would use any means possible to destroy me. Inflicting marital deaths and intense suffering failed to turn me against God. Of course Satan would use broken Christians to niggle in and try to destroy my faith, crush my spirit, and claim me for the pits of hell.

Satan is the author of lies and doubt, shame and bondage. His newest afflictions burdened my already weakened heart and soul.

For a time.

And then I rose up and became very protective of my relationship with God. Instead of stabbing elephants, I started stabbing legalism and that Pharisee complex. I grew stronger in my faith despite anyone's attempts to put me in bondage.

I absolutely refused to put Ed back on my shoulders and rebuked any suggestion to do so. Our divorce took eighteen months to finalize (that's a long funeral) and many took it upon themselves to "set me straight" before "it was too late."

Every time a broken Christian judged and condemned me, I felt like they were saying Jesus died for everyone's sins...except mine. It was as if they believed Jesus died for every sin...except divorce. And that God couldn't handle my divorce—my divorce was bigger than God. I felt as though they were telling me to climb up that cross and remove my sin from Christ's shoulders and tell Him, "Never mind, Lord. I'll carry this myself."

It infuriated me, and when it started infuriating me, Satan lost his power to push me down into that pit.

BROKEN umbrellas

For every hurtful encounter, God supplied glorious encounters. For every nasty look, condemning remark, and ungodly action, God gave from the depths of His own heart to meet my emotional and spiritual needs.

Those godly sources I mentioned earlier—Bible studies, praying friends, yearly retreats—remained steadfast in my darkest hour. It was a battle, literally, between these godly Christians and the ungodly ones. It wasn't until the odds teetered in favor of the godly influence that I was able to stand (in Christ) among the wreckage and claim complete deliverance.

God rebuilt my pile of dust into the strongest foundation on which He constructed—and continues to construct—His temple. A temple of faith, integrity, perseverance, and noble character. He turned my ashes into beauty (Isaiah 61:3). Without my past—that rebuilt foundation—I would not be here with you now, free from *all* the chains that once held me captive.

Let not the opinions of man interfere with the directions given to you by God.[6] ~ Jarrid Wilson

fourteen

step

under

BROKEN umbrellas

Whatever can be heaped on painful fires to keep them burning, our enemy is always willing to supply. All he needs are people who have not committed themselves to God's plan, to his purposes, and to being filled with God's nature.[7]

Emma Broch Stuart

Jill Briscoe, in her book, *It Had to Be a Monday*, talks about suffering and how Satan uses that to his advantage to make a crisis worse. It exposes the nature of the human heart when a hurting situation is made worse by the actions of others. Jill Briscoe uses the example of price increases on basic items after a natural disaster. But it's very relevant to the crisis—and suffering—of divorce.

So why do folks fixate on divorce and treat it as the biggest, most unforgivable sin? They'll jump right over gossip, pride, or arrogance in order to correct and chastise someone who has gotten a divorce. Completely detour lust and pornography, lying and abuse to thump their Bible upside the head of someone seeking divorce. We have turned divorce into an idol. An idol is anything that takes our focus off God. Our focus is most certainly not on God when we are shaking our finger in a divorced person's face.

Relationships have also become an idol. When our focus is on gluing the broken pieces of a relationship back together instead of seeking God's healing for each individual, we are no longer focused on God. We are focused on religion.

Larry Crabb, in his book *Soultalk: Speaking with Power into the Lives of Others*, shares an example of a couple who comes to him for counseling. The husband has deeply hurt his wife by having an affair. Crabb questions our vision for this marriage. Do we want restoration of the marriage first and foremost? If so, this requires religious advice because it is a religious vision. Crabb goes on to explain that working toward restoring two souls allows us to move toward the Holy Spirit. This is priority, and from that flows everything good—like their restored marriage.[8]

It makes so much sense if we just let that soak into us for a minute. Why would we ever aim for a couple's restored marriage if the individuals themselves aren't healed first?

Stay at all costs. Increase intimacy. Forgive. Submit. Stay.

BROKEN umbrellas

Those religious leaders during the end times covered me with their broken umbrellas—and instead of receiving protection, I got drenched.

We relate and serve, love and protect with our brokenness.

Oh, but when we are covered with God's umbrella, we are accepted and safe. We have but to step under, and His protection shelters us.

Images are so powerful. I can close my eyes and picture God's umbrella. It shimmers as it shields. Golden frame, canopy that sparkles, the handle just the right size for the hand of God. And it's big. Solid. Not flimsy and bendable. It's made to shelter—no matter whether we're standing, kneeling, or scattered in a million pieces. His sturdy umbrella is *the* haven from any storm.

Investing in broken people reaps glorious rewards for the kingdom. Marriage means little if it doesn't glorify God. This is why I'm so passionate about broken people. Patching up a couple with wobbling towers—to ease our conscience that we've done our part to fix their marriage—does not glorify God. Sitting amongst the rubble with a broken person as they sift through the debris—speaking love and truth into their life as God rebuilds, crying with them, praying over them, listening—*does* glorify God.

He will cover you with his feathers. He will shelter you with his wings. His faithful promises are your armor and protection (Psalm 91:4).

fifteen

dangling

bitter

grapes

BROKEN umbrellas

I meant that you are not to associate with anyone who claims to be a believer yet indulges in sexual sin, or is greedy, or worships idols, or is abusive, or is a drunkard, or cheats people. Don't even eat with such people (1 Corinthians 5:11).

I'm not sure I've made a smooth transition from broken Christians back to Ed, but we do need to cover that 18-month-long funeral and the layers of confusion and hurt that overwhelmed me. As more of my healing is revealed, we'll circle back around to the brokenness of religious abuse.

So, I'm nestled in my apartment, navigating singlehood in a foreign country, dealing with the effects of many horrendous marital deaths, grieving, and dodging those tornadoes. It's a wonder I even found the strength to get out of bed in the morning.

But I did. One morning at a time. It took a while before my little leaves unfurled and grew toward the sun (or the Son). For the longest time, Ed—though separated and knee deep in divorce proceedings—continued to pluck my itty bitty bean.

For example, he almost kissed me one afternoon while dropping our daughter off after a weekend visit. I froze as he intimately cupped my chin, hesitating just inches from my lips before moving to greet me with a kiss on the cheek (as is customary in France). For days, this confused me, frightened me, and had me on edge until a sister in Christ prayed with me and counseled me. Apparently, I had boundary issues. Who would have guessed?

I was able to confront him and inquire as to what prompted this almost-kiss. He admitted it was the lack of intimate touching in his life, and that he had not changed his mind about the divorce. I was able to set clear boundaries with him. I credit God for that burst of strength. Bursts of strength like this are what sustained me through months and months of grieving and the intense pain that comes with healing.

Things like that almost-kiss were what left me withering, struggling to grow. *Pluck, grow, unfurl, pluck!* Combine that with the ungodly tornadoes, and I was assaulted on all fronts.

Before I rose up and started stabbing legalism and rebuking

BROKEN umbrellas

suggestions to put Ed back on my shoulders, I was gripped with fear that God might ask me to go back into this broken marriage. I clung to a small group of godly women who literally held my arms up for me in prayer because I was too weak to do it myself.

One woman gave me the most reassuring wisdom that immediately flooded me with peace. She told me not to fear, that God would not ask me to enter that brokenness again. That if our marriage was to be restored, Ed would be a completely different person. Our marriage would be completely different. I would be completely different. God's work in each of us—and in turn the marriage—would be so glorious, that I would enter with thanksgiving because God orchestrated it.

I still struggled with bitterness, and the mental back and forth nearly crushed me. Waiting on a court date, yet wondering if God was working in the direction of two restored people, thus a restored marriage. I dangled there for months, hanging like a cluster of bitter grapes.

The dangling was necessary. I see that now. I learned so much while hanging there. I learned that during the end times with Ed, my focus was on the relationship, and at times, it took my focus off God. I focused more on how much Ed was hurting me with his sin than on how much Ed was hurting God with his sin. And I never considered how my nagging hurt God.

I also learned that I was hiding behind Ed's decision to divorce rather than change. For years he had hidden behind my skirts, afraid of taking responsibility for anything. After leaving the "marriage home," I realized Ed's choice to divorce rather than change actually relieved me, and I even journaled that it would be nice to let him take the fall for once.

Did God let me get away with that? Of course not! While I was in this period of grieving, dealing with bitterness, standing up to tornadoes, and gathering baby spurts of strength, God was working on my character. And he refused to let me be a coward—just like God wouldn't let Jacob be a coward in Genesis

31 when he was fleeing Laban.

Even though God delivered Jacob from Laban, Jacob still had to confront Laban. God used this passage to show me that I was being a coward and my character was more important than who actually filed for divorce. Wanting this to fall on Ed only proved I was more concerned with appearances than seeking God.

Francis Chan, in his book *Crazy Love*, says, "We're willing to make changes in our lives only if we think it affects our salvation." He says this is why he has so many people asking him questions like, "Can I divorce my wife and still go to heaven?" Chan goes on to say, "To me, these questions are tragic because they reveal much about the state of our hearts. They demonstrate that our concern is more about going to heaven than loving the King."[9]

God convicted my heart about hiding behind Ed. I pushed through with the divorce and it fell on my shoulders—actually, it fell on Christ's shoulders.

sixteen

blame

game

BROKEN umbrellas

When the cool evening breezes were blowing, the man and his wife heard the Lord God walking about in the garden. So they hid from the Lord God among the trees. Then the Lord God called to the man, "Where are you?" He replied, "I heard you walking in the garden, so I hid. I was afraid because I was naked." "Who told you that you were naked?" the Lord God asked. "Have you eaten from the tree whose fruit I commanded you not to eat?" The man replied, "It was the woman you gave me who gave me the fruit, and I ate it." Then the Lord God asked the woman, "What have you done?" "The serpent deceived me," she replied. "That's why I ate it" (Genesis 3:8-13).

Christ was chosen to be our Savior, even before the creation of the world (1 Peter 1:20). Therefore, any one of us, put in Adam or Eve's position, would have given in to what Satan offered. We do it now by placing other things higher than God. When sin entered the world, it set into motion an unalterable series of consequences that generation upon generation would feel for all of life on this earth. We focus more on the game than we do on the score which is:

Jesus: everything

Us: nothing

Any relationship where God is not the focus is a broken relationship. People store up relational treasures here on earth, and if God isn't central to those nuggets, then it's a storehouse kept in vain. Ecclesiastes 1:2 says that "everything is meaningless!"

Couples doing decades of life together is an astounding thing. I'm awestruck when I hear stories of overcoming loss and sorrow, struggling through hardships, growing old together, and creating a legacy of commitment that reaches beyond the boundaries of a society known for its disposability. Yet, which is more astounding: a newly married couple who puts Christ first in their relationship; or a couple who have been married 20 years and don't put Christ first in their relationship? Without Christ, everything is meaningless!

I no longer blame Ed for our broken marriage. I blame Satan. Ephesians 6:12 says, "For our struggle is not against flesh and blood, but against the rulers, against the authorities, against the powers of this dark world and against the spiritual forces of evil in the heavenly realms" (NIV).

Satan wars for my soul—as well as Ed's—and uses any means possible to turn my focus from God. He prowls the earth like a roaring lion, seeking to devour (1 Peter 5:8). We must stay rooted in God, lest we fall victim to his tactics. And they are

BROKEN umbrellas

subtle. They appear as truth. They appear godly and biblical. Satan quoted Scripture when he tempted Jesus in Matthew 4. Jesus, the Son of God! How much more will Satan do to capture you and me in his snares?

When we are unhealthy, broken inside, carrying baggage from our past and the world on our shoulders, we are quick to blame. I said earlier that I couldn't carry my son's sin on my shoulders and didn't even realize I was carrying Ed's. Maybe we can't carry blame when our burden is already heavy. Maybe we can't take responsibility because the weight of everything else is too hard to bear. I think about Ed and those end times when he refused to take responsibility for anything. Maybe he couldn't. With the sin he was already packing around, it's safe to assume there was no more room to carry responsibility.

Also, we are creatures who naturally dodge the guilt bullet. We resist being at fault. Just reread the exchange between God and Adam and Eve. Excuses. There's always a good reason why something is not our fault.

I don't think I have ever talked to a divorced person who didn't blame their spouse for the divorce. A true sign of brokenness is when we can't see fault within ourselves, or when someone really is at fault and relief floods us. We're glad it's them and not us. Until it happens to us. Just analyse your reaction the next time you see someone pulled over for speeding. I dare you to pull in behind and ask the officer to give you a ticket too because just a mile back, you had been speeding.

We would never do that, would we? Yet we are all guilty of speeding. We just don't always get caught.

We are all guilty of sins that tear apart a marriage. We just don't always have DIVORCE branded on our relationship resumes.

The blame game is a "holier than thou" approach to broken people—a Pharisee approach to broken people. It distances us from God's plan for our lives or the impact we can make in other people's lives.

seventeen

rain check

BROKEN umbrellas

When religion fuels our beliefs, we obey God, hoping to be accepted. When the gospel of Jesus Christ is the foundation of our beliefs, we are accepted, and this cultivates obedience.

With every life lesson I learned—every nugget of wisdom I gained—I thought God was finished with me and I was healed. He proved me wrong time and time again. I had a long way to go.

Let me say again: it's a journey. I discovered that if I rushed ahead, I had to learn the same lessons over again. But God halted one harmful relational habit that deserves some attention. It was another pivotal area of my healing. And more than anything else, God wants me to be vulnerable with you about this.

After some of the shock wore off in those first several months of being on my own, and after I knew God was indeed delivering me from my broken marriage (no more mental back and forth), I anticipated the day I could start dating. The end times—though married—were some of the loneliest years I've ever endured. I still clung, subconsciously, to the belief that a new relationship would fix the hurts from past relationships. I started an innocent friendship with a gentleman who I thought was a Christian. When this gentleman invited me to dinner, I took a rain check because my divorce wasn't final. See? Being a single Christian wasn't so hard. I didn't see any harm though in engaging in conversations to feel him out and see what we had in common.

I discovered through conversations that he was not yet a Christian, though he was attending a church. I found myself "discipling" him and was uncomfortable doing so. The Bible says not to be yoked to an unbeliever (2 Corinthians 6:14), but I thought I could get him "Christian enough" before the divorce was finalized if I could engage a brother in Christ to take over discipling him.

I took a sister in Christ with me to meet with this brother and explained the situation. He listened, accepted to take this gentleman under his wing, and then he said, "Let's talk about you for a minute." He proceeded to counsel me, asking me if I'd given myself enough time to heal [from those marital deaths]. I explained how lonely I had been for so long and that God had

BROKEN umbrellas

taught me a lot and I felt ready. God created me for relationship. I was eager to see how a healthy one functioned. He asked me if I even liked this gentleman. I told him I didn't know yet.

My brother in Christ explained that accepting an invitation to dinner—rain check or otherwise—implied that I already considered him marriage material. I panicked. *No way!* I insisted this was not the case, and that I thought dating was the process for considering.

He also shared a story with me about a friend who waited a year after her divorce before dating to give herself time to heal and discover the direction God was leading her. I balked at that. A year? *No way!* This brother in Christ was so respectful and caring. He suggested I take this to God and then he lifted me up in prayer right then and there.

And God spoke to my unhealthy heart. He wanted thirteen months of my undivided attention. He called me into a "relationship fast"—and it was even *more* than a year. *No way!*

Yes way!

And as you will see in a couple of chapters, it was during my time in the "cave of fasting" that deep-rooted brokenness was healed and I unlearned broken ways of relating. But first, let's spend a little time talking about how God equipped and strengthened me for the cave of fasting.

eighteen

rope

holders

BROKEN umbrellas

One day Jesus was teaching in a house, *and the healing power of the Lord was with Him. Pharisees and religious scholars were sitting and listening, having come from villages all across the regions of Galilee and Judea and from* the holy city of Jerusalem. *Some men came* to the house, *carrying a paralyzed man on his bed pallet. They wanted to bring him in and present him to Jesus, but the house was so packed with people that they couldn't get in. So they climbed up on the roof and pulled off some roof tiles. Then they lowered the man* by ropes *so he came to rest right in front of Jesus. In this way, their faith was visible to Jesus* (Luke 5:17-20 The Voice).

Arriving is a glorious feeling. We made it out of those murky waters. I've hinted to this moment throughout the previous chapters—rising above, gathering strength, inevitable growth, and calm waters. If we read everything to this point without the glimpses of healing and restoration, it would be hopeless and sobering stuff. I can't imagine anyone going through heaps and heaps of heartbreak, crises, grieving, chaos, marital deaths, tornadoes, or losing a grandbaby without Christ by their side.

Jesus is my hero, there is no doubt about it. I'm sobbing again. I really want you to get this. More than I wanted you to grasp how deep that pit was, I want you to grasp how amazing God is. Those trials shaped me into the person I am today. I claim all of them for the glory of God. While at the time it felt as though they would crush me, I wouldn't give back, trade, or share any of them now for anything. Those trials were stamped with the Royal Seal of God, and when something is stamped with God's Royal Seal, you can be sure it is used to mold your character—if you let it.

While God didn't "take those cups of suffering from me" (Luke 22:42), He did remain at my side through it all. My faith was stretched and tested, and I grew. I didn't stay shriveled up in defeat, self-pity, or anger. My spiritual roots grew deeper, my head aligned with my heart. Each trial, calamity, and *death*, only proved God more and more trustworthy and faithful.

I said before that God gave from the depths of His own heart to meet my needs. He did this in many ways. I'd like to share some of them with you, the first being the most profound. My rope holders.

Let's travel back and walk beside the man whose friends are taking him to see Jesus. I can visualize his bed pallet and friends surrounding it, holding the ropes as they carry him to Jesus. Did a crowded house persuade them to give up their mission? No. They went above and beyond the call of friendship, showed *hesed*, and devised a plan: climb up on the roof, tear a hole in the

BROKEN umbrellas

tile, and lower their friend down in front of Jesus. How many holes do you think they made before they found the exact spot where Jesus was?

Sometimes I wish Bible writers had elaborated on some of those stories. But that doesn't stop me from imagining. I can hear their conversation. Which rope holder would take the lead as they lugged their friend up to the roof? One of them wipes the sweat from his brow—it had to be hot up there—while he watches the roof tiles being removed. Another rope holder pats his paralyzed friend on the shoulder, reassuring him. Their determination touches me deeply. Their character is worthy of awe.

I myself have some determined rope holders. If not for their perseverance, their *hesed*—faithful—love, and their character, I would not have found myself lowered before Jesus, or experienced His healing power over my broken life. God handpicked each precious rope holder and placed them in my path for such a time as to bring me before my Savior for complete healing.

They glorified God by sitting amongst the rubble with me as I sifted through the debris—they spoke love and truth into my life as God rebuilt. They cried with me, encouraged, counseled, and loved on me. They surrounded me in prayer, laid hands on me, and carried me to the foot of the cross countless times. They never gave up on me, and they never let me turn from God.

From the small group who were hands-on, to the praying group in California, and everyone in between, I praise God for these rope holders. I am so humbled to have received such an outpouring of Jesus in my desperate and critical time of need.

There's a special place in God's heart for the rope holders of the world. They are precious in His sight. And I am indeed blessed beyond measure to have them in my life.

nineteen

gloriously

equipped

BROKEN umbrellas

It's one thing to desire wholeness, it's another thing entirely to know how to be whole—how to get from where you are to where God wants you to be. Give a broken person the tools and knowledge to find healing, and he or she can do amazing things. And the most amazing of all is that the entire process leads to a deeper knowing of our Creator. That is wholeness.

Another outpouring of God from His own heart was the opportunity to gain knowledge and wisdom through a school of ministry.[10] I gleaned in those fields for many months—and still glean from that gleaning to this day. I learned so much about God. I discovered who I am, and more importantly, who I am not.

Six Saturdays—with mounds of glorious homework in between—gave me seminary-level teaching that became the concrete God used to rebuild my foundation. The fields I gleaned in were: learning conflict resolution; how to build a ministry project from the ground up; and the history of women in the Church.

Professors taught on spiritual warfare, studying the Bible, and people-helping skills. Every drop soaked into my parched soul. The school of ministry gave me assurance as I grew in my faith as well as confidence and knowledge as a follower of Christ standing in the Word of God. Some of God's best "iron sharpening iron" (Proverbs 27:17) happens when God's people gather to learn more about Him.

At the close of the school, each student was asked to write a letter to future students. I'd like to share mine with you:

> *My heart is bursting to share with you all that God has done for me through the school of ministry. I came into the school a broken, pitiful mess. Uneducated and full of shame, wondering why on earth I was even participating. I would never gain enough wisdom or maturity to do anything for God's kingdom. And now? Well, I'm still broken in some places. But my shame is GONE! Replaced by incredible grace. Knowledge and courage, they fill me. It is with boldness that I step out for God and obediently open my heart to hear His call on my life. The school of ministry taught me who God*

BROKEN umbrellas

is, who I am, and what happens when those two combine to make something gloriously equipped for kingdom purposes.

During that first Saturday of teaching, the afternoon professor used the book *The Gift of Being Yourself* by David G. Benner as a homework assignment to emphasize the qualities and character of a leader. I was profoundly touched by this sentence in the book: "In Christian spiritual transformation, the self that embarks on the journey is not the self that arrives."[11]

I realized the profoundness of this immediately, from the few months God had been working on rebuilding my foundation to arriving at this assignment. I realized it again at the completion of the school, by how much knowledge and truth I learned. I realize it sitting here with you, reliving my past, and sharing my healing. And I will realize it again when I arrive at heaven's gate.

It's a journey—and it is all for God's glory. He's the one constructing His temple through me. He's the one who used my past to shape my foundation on which everything else is built. He's the one who holds my present and my future in His hands. He even decides the very next breath I take.

This same professor challenged the students to write a Who Am I paper without listing what we "do." I'd also like to share this with you:

Who Am I

- **I am a mess.** A Jesus-freak mess.
  (And I praise God for loving me in spite of it.)
- **I am a control freak.**
  (I have nothing to add to this one. Control freak pretty much says it all.)
- **I am an obsessive fixer.**
  (This is negative in that I am unable to move on

until I have exhausted everything in my power to fix something I have messed up.)

And **I am working on** all these things **through Christ** who strengthens me.

- **I am a daughter of the King.**
  (Who doesn't deserve to even polish my crown, let alone wear it. But wear it I do with humble pride and deep gratitude.)
- **I am a wallflower** who takes time to smell the flowers.
- **I am in love** with my Savior and heavenly Father.
  (And awed at everything He created.)
- **I am a crier.**
  (A snorting sobber is more like it, and it doesn't take much to get me going. Just a song about Christ. Or a flower swaying in the breeze, created delicately by the Most High's gentle touch.)
- **I am an organizer and list maker.**
  (Ha! Just look at the format of this "Who Am I" paper.)
- **I am hospitable, caring, and eager to serve.**
  (My humble door is always open.)

And **I am** all these things **through Christ** who strengthens me.

Those points on control freak and obsessive fixer are painful to read. Oh, how I have grown since writing this paper. Now I let Him be the Glue that fixes what needs fixing. I admit that I'm still a snorting sobber. (Ha!)

BROKEN umbrellas

Now I pause in everything and look for His mighty hand. And my favorite question is, "What does God want me to learn from this?"

It puts us in the perfect position for obedience and growth when we can change our question from, "Why?" to "For what purpose?"

Because there is always a purpose. Nothing is wasted with God.

I'd like to conclude this chapter on being gloriously equipped by sharing pieces from one final paper I wrote near the end of the school when asked to describe a difficult situation in my life when God didn't do what I was hoping, praying, and expecting He would do:

> *To say the final years of my marriage was a difficult situation is an understatement. To say that God didn't do what I was hoping, praying, and expecting is also an understatement. I hoped He would change my husband. I prayed Ed would suddenly start loving me and stop neglecting me. I expected our marriage to survive because after all, we were Christians.*
>
> *What I believed about God and His clear message about divorce affected my situation; I felt I had to stay and suffer this horrible crucifixion because Christ had endured far worse than what I was enduring.*
>
> *What I learned about the importance of theology in this situation is that God's love for me is unchanging. That He does deliver us from bad situations and He does say, "Enough is enough."*

Emma Broch Stuart

I learned that restoring my heart to Christ is far more important than restoring my marriage to an unfaithful mate.

God delivered me from *this horrible situation. But He also delivered me* for *other things. Things He reveals to me tenderly and in His time.*

I pray this resonates deeply: God doesn't deliver us *from* situations so we can be on our merry way. He delivers us *for* situations that glorify Him.

twenty

neon

lights

BROKEN umbrellas

I need barn doors to swing wide open and neon lights to flash "This way! This way!" That's my confirmation style, and for a season, God obliged. He delighted in pulling open those barn doors that creaked on rusty hinges and plugging in the neon lights that guided me down the right path. As my spiritual roots grow, He doesn't open those barn doors as wide, nor does He always plug in the neon lights. But He never fails to confirm no matter how many times I ask. He delights in showing me His goodness. And He delights in me when my spiritual eyes can spot His confirmation no matter how it arrives, whether flashing and stampeding through a barn door, or fluttering on a butterfly wing.[12]

I thought it would be fun to spend a chapter talking about how God confirmed that He wanted me to write *Broken Umbrellas*.

Two months into the relationship fast—nine months into the funeral—I attended my fourth annual weekend retreat. The three previous ones, I'd gone seeking strength to return and face my troubled marriage. This was the first retreat where I went seeking personal growth, not strength to maintain. I realized this a few days before the retreat and rested in that peace, allowing myself to be blessed even before going.

Keep in mind that divorce proceedings were in full swing. I found out the day I left for the retreat that Ed had received another batch of papers from my lawyer and vowed revenge for some concerns I had stipulated about visitation of our daughter. Ed's vowed revenge worried me, and I carried that into the retreat. When I arrived, I immediately sought out the prayer leader and scheduled a prayer appointment with her for the following morning. This prayer leader just so happened to be one of my rope holders from California who pledged the year before to lift me up in prayer on a regular basis.

Between the time I scheduled the appointment and the following morning, God spoke to my heart that this was a distraction. My anxiety immediately vanished. I cancelled my prayer appointment. I told the prayer leader—my rope holder who was already aware of my situation—that I did not want to pray for this; the prayers already going into heaven covered my current worries.

A few months leading up to the retreat, I felt God prompting me to write about my brokenness. So, days before, when I realized I was going for personal growth, I asked God to confirm that He indeed wanted me to write *Broken Umbrellas*.

I asked my mom to pray I would receive confirmation at the retreat. She asked if I'd recognize it if God gave it to me. Though I felt I would, doubt crept into my heart.

BROKEN umbrellas

So, at the retreat, I waited and waited to feel that God chill race up my spine, causing me to gasp. As the retreat neared an end, I wondered if God had changed how He spoke to me and was trying the "subtle" approach. I wanted neon lights to flash, "This way!" *That* is the confirmation style I needed. I envisioned someone—or multiple someones—coming up to me and verbally confirming that I was supposed to write about brokenness.

Then a sister in Christ pulled me aside the last morning and said, "Emma, God wants me to tell you something and I don't want to. I have avoided it, but I don't feel I can any longer. I have to say this, and I don't know how you'll take it."

Butterflies did their flittery dance in my stomach. This was it! I knew it! She was going to say the words I needed to hear. My confirmation was about to roll off her tongue.

She said, "God wants you to know that the man who threw you away will regret it."

She did not know the details of my impending divorce. I was shocked; and I cried. I wanted to hear confirmation on my writing project, but I so desperately needed to hear this too. Her words felt like closure—that solid kind that says, "Carry no more shame." It was like God closing the chapter on Ed and confirming that I was there for personal growth and *not* marriage/divorce issues.

God decided what He wanted to confirm. I wondered if He was saying, "I am not going to give you confirmation on writing a book, but I am going to give you this." I surrendered in complete trust that He knew what I needed. I immediately let go of my "want" for confirmation concerning the book and just basked in the blessings of what God revealed. I left that retreat a different person, at peace with the knowledge that either I did not get my confirmation, and that was okay; or I did (and God changed His love language to me) and I missed it. I prayed He would send it again if that was the case.

Earlier in the retreat, another precious rope holder from California told me she had something for my daughter and gave me a cute little yellow sack with two wrapped presents inside. She said, "These are to put in your suitcase." Which I did that night right before bed. I noticed one was for me and smiled as I packed it, thinking I would appreciate it more when I wasn't so tired.

Retreat duties pulled us apart, and we didn't get any quality visiting time. When I got home, I opened my gift. A writing journal. Guess what immediately raced up my spine? Yup, you guessed it! That God chill. I gasped and started crying. My confirmation had been sitting in my suitcase all weekend. I cried for hours, praising God.

He is so generous and extravagant. He didn't just give me confirmation, He gave it through someone very dear to me, and in a tangible way that verbal confirmation simply couldn't measure up to.

I phoned this precious rope holder and shared God's blessing with her. She was beyond delighted to be the vehicle in which my confirmation arrived. She said she searched for just the right gift to bring me, struggling over several things, and then found this journal and it hit her. This was weeks before I even asked for confirmation.

Jesus says in Matthew 6:8, "Your Father knows exactly what you need even before you ask him!"

In the end, God gave me more than I ever asked for, and it was just the encouragement I needed to forge ahead. The perfect reminder that God is trustworthy.

twenty-one

cave

of

fasting

BROKEN umbrellas

The discipline of fasting from one thing doesn't deprive us. Rather, it allows us the incredible opportunity to feast on something else. God prepares the table, invites us to join Him, and we partake of all He offers.

It's important to understand that God doesn't call us to anything He hasn't first equipped us to handle. Without my rope holders and without the ongoing knowledge I was gaining from the school of ministry, I would never have had the courage to devote my undivided attention to God in this way. It was the biggest act of trust I have ever displayed, giving God my loneliness and trusting Him to carry me through—and healing me in the process.

With that said, I have also experienced God asking me to step out in faith without being equipped first, trusting He will supply what I need as I need it—not always *before* I need it. I can't say it enough, it's a journey. He knows we need to crawl before we can walk. And He would never ask us to run until we conquer crawling and walking.

I praise God for giving my brother in Christ the courage to counsel me when I didn't ask for it. Many times we are silent because we feel it's none of our business. If God leads, speak up! I am forever thankful he did. He was instrumental in bringing me to a place where I heard God's voice about this. While it is utterly embarrassing to share my brokenness with you in this book, it would be horrifying to omit it and someone reading this needed to hear it.

It scared me to realize I had fallen back into the same pattern of seeking companionship while still carrying baggage. God used that to nudge me into this relationship fast. I went kicking my feet just a little, but only because I thought I could learn what I needed to learn in a shorter amount of time. Thirteen months seemed so long!

God had already proven Himself trustworthy over and over. I chose to trust He must know how much time I needed. I embraced that as I stood at the opening to the "cave" and watched the last rays of sunlight streak across the horizon. Then I settled in with God around a fire. I admit, I feared the unknown. I

BROKEN umbrellas

didn't know what He had planned for me, but I knew it involved unlearning the damaging relational concepts deeply embedded in my heart and soul.

We don't always know God's purposes until we surrender to His will no matter what. Until we arrive at the place where we trust that He knows best for our life and obediently follow, no matter where He leads. If we knew the purpose and then decided to follow, trusting Him wouldn't be necessary.

Interestingly enough, one of my homework assignments for the school of ministry was to choose a spiritual discipline and put it into practice. This aligned perfectly with my relationship fast, and I chose the spiritual discipline "Simplicity and Fasting." I don't believe in coincidence. I truly believe God orchestrates these alignings.

I pause here to flip through the pages of my journal. I don't know what to share first! It's true I've given you glimpses of the wisdom I gained, but there is so much more. Chronological order is not going to work. I think we'll divide those nuggets of wisdom and healing into categories and work through each one. Why don't we put them on slips of paper, mix them up in a hat, and draw them out one at a time?

twenty-two

gently

broken

BROKEN umbrellas

Every person I've met who really seems liberated to love, enjoy, and obey God as a lifestyle has been on the battlefield. They usually appreciate and apply victory more readily because they've experienced the misery of defeat firsthand.[13]

Just the thought of change can evoke fear. Fear can cripple us and keep us from even taking the first step to change—which is acknowledging that change is needed. We fear losing control, and we fear revealing our true self because more than likely we don't even know who our true self is. We fear what others think about us. We fear leaving our comfort zone no matter how toxic that zone is—it's ours and it's comfort. This is why people find themselves in a cycle of mistakes—repeating the same ones over and over. It's what they know.

I feared the unknown. Everything I had experienced in my life prior to the cave of fasting was known. But I craved God more than I feared the unknown. I craved knowledge and truth, and that deep longing pushed fear aside.

The first thing I felt led to do during this fast was to journal past relationships. Nothing drawn-out, just an overview of each one. Patterns emerged; and God began the long process of gently breaking habits and beliefs that had settled in the deepest parts of my being.

When we have been wounded, something is broken. I soon realized that in order to be restored to relational health, something must be broken in the healing process. Being wounded or being restored, breaking takes place.

But being broken by God and being broken by people are two entirely different things. Being broken by people—Satan's weapon—attacks who you are. Being broken by God *reveals* who you are.

How can we tell the difference? Satan using people—including ourselves—to break us always involves shame and bitterness. His voice is always degrading and attacks our soul and our mind. Satan always brings up our past in order to hold us down and fill us with discouragement. This produces internal chaos and breeds hopelessness. He attacks us with words that belittle us, condemn us, and insist we are worthless.

When God breaks us, it is always with a gentle voice. Though

BROKEN umbrellas

letting go of harmful habits can be painful, His voice brings peace and hope. He never shakes a finger at us, rather holds out His hand to us. God stirs our spirit and prompts our heart. He shows us where we fail and forgives us when we repent. Then He forgets. God reveals to us that the world does not name us. Nor does it claim us. We are His beloved. And God gave us His Word that we may compare our personal revelations with what He says in the Bible.

> *All Scripture is inspired by God and is useful to teach us what is true and to make us realize what is wrong in our lives. It corrects us when we are wrong and teaches us to do what is right. God uses it to prepare and equip his people to do every good work* (2 Timothy 3:16-17).

First Corinthians 11:23-24 tells us, "[Jesus] took the bread *in His hands*; and after giving thanks *to God*, He broke it and said, 'This is My body, *broken* for you. Keep doing this so that you *and all who come after* will have a vivid reminder of Me'" (The Voice).

Jesus gave us this beautiful symbol of His body broken on the cross for our sins. This "breaking" brought us salvation. God breaking our brokenness brings healing and restoration.

Drawing me into this relationship fast was in fact part of the breaking. He never stops breaking His children of sinful habits or harmful behaviors. It's that whole process of perfecting something imperfect. It's a journey.

Truth be told, I didn't even have the confidence to enter another relationship. Before entering the fast, I was only going through the motions because that's what I knew. I now realize my lack of confidence was from not knowing who I was in Christ.

One tool God used to teach me who I am in Christ was the Bible study *Breaking Free: The Journey, The Stories* by Beth Moore. It was instrumental in delivering me of many false beliefs I had about myself and dug up deep roots of brokenness in my life. Beth Moore taught me that my truth (my past) plus Satan's lies equalled captivity. Only when I partnered my truth with God's truth (forgiveness) did I truly know freedom.

A shocking revelation from doing this Bible study: In the past, I had replaced God with relationships. As a Christian, I had continued to idolize relationships because my focus was on getting them glued back together instead of getting my soul restored.

Only after being imprisoned did I truly know freedom.

That sentence needs to sit alone and simmer in our hearts. We all have wounds that need to be healed. We may not even know it because we've become so familiar with imprisonment. But only after the process of breaking that wound (brokenness) can we truly know freedom in Christ (restoration).

Ground must be broken to plant grain. Clouds must break for rain to fall on the grain. Grain must be broken to make flour. Bread must be broken to give us nourishment.[14]

Remember, being broken by God and being broken by people are two entirely different things. Being broken by people—Satan's weapon—attacks who you are. Being broken by God *reveals* who you are.

twenty-three stones of abuse

BROKEN umbrellas

The huge stone of legalism has been rolled from my life, but the little pebbles that remain—or sneak in—will create a stone. God and I work diligently to remove the pebbles and replace the roughness—big or small—with the gentleness of God's truth and love.

Religious abuse is both difficult to endure and difficult to diagnose. Remember in the previous chapter how we described God's voice and the difference between being broken by people and being broken by God? We can determine God speaking through Christians by the same standards. It is a hand being offered, not a finger being shaken. It is "Have you thought about" instead of "You better watch out." It is the fruit of the Spirit—words and encouragement offered with love, peace, and gentleness.

I don't want to spend a lot of time on this subject. My main reason for including this chapter is because I can't let you leave this book believing the worst about God's people who inflicted legalism on me.

God can meet them where they are and harvest a crop of understanding and more characteristics of Christ. We are all on this journey, each of us at a different place. We each bring to that journey our past, our brokenness, our beliefs, and our experiences.

Again, it's the process of perfecting the imperfect.

God used my encounters with legalism to bring awareness that religious abuse exists, but also to ripen the fruit of the spirit within myself for relating to broken people. Those harmful pokes by Christians forced me to stand up for myself and for my relationship with Christ. Legalism drove me to search for answers within the pages of God's Word.

And it turned me into the arms of my rope holders who persevered in loving me. These rope holders, too, have their imperfections as they continue along their journey, but God also meets them where they are.

If the sharp edges of an imperfect Christian have rubbed against you, pray for them. Maybe God is calling you to be an instrument in His plan to restore and heal them. Grace is amazing. And just as God gives it to us, we need to give it to

BROKEN umbrellas

others.

Now that God has delivered me from that pit, I am able to see the passion in some of these sharp-edged Christians in their pursuit of me. I could only feel the pain from their words and actions while I was in the pit, but now I see their love—though it was delivered imperfectly.

We must be on guard for the pebbles of legalism that get thrown into our path. We are all susceptible to this subtle disease. Balance must be found in our relationships with others so we aren't stepping on hearts when we step in their pit to sit with them. God calls us to use discernment when inputting into another's life, and our words should be gracious.

> *Let your conversation be always full of grace, seasoned with salt, so that you may know how to answer everyone* (Colossians 4:6 NIV).

Another fiery trap is something called *obstructionism*. From a Christian point of view, obstructionists often masquerade as godly, helpful, even nonjudgmental. But they withhold tangible blessings from you because they deem you undeserving. Feeling threatened by your growth, they attempt to "obstruct" God's work in your life. Obstructionists often suffer from passive-aggressive disorder.

The story of Jonah the prophet comes to mind when looking for examples of obstructionism. When God told the prophet to go to the wicked city of Nineveh and preach, Jonah ran. He considered the Ninevites undeserving of God's mercy. Jonah thought he could obstruct God's plans by running.

God showed me very quickly that His plans for my life cannot be thwarted by obstructionism or legalism. He also reminded me that our battle is not with people, it's with Satan.

If we abide in Him, He abides in us (John 15:4). *That is*

our weapon for destroying both of these spiritual diseases. Remaining in Him so we know His voice. The more we hear God's voice, the easier it is to recognize when it's not.

twenty-four

pleasant

boundaries

BROKEN umbrellas

The boundary lines have fallen for me in pleasant places (Psalm 16:6 NIV).

A neighbor and I used to walk together every afternoon to pick up our children from school. We had daughters in the same class. One day, my neighbor spent our five-minute walk explaining how she had cheated the government out of money many years ago. I asked her how she felt about this and whether or not she thought she'd ever be caught. She was confident enough time had gone by and she was in the clear; besides, she felt entitled to that money.

A few months later, during our walk, she informed me that my daughter was friends with the class thief and I needed to put an end to their friendship. I explained that my daughter and I didn't believe in judging the person, only the crime, and I refused to make my daughter stop being friends with someone rumored to be the class thief.

My neighbor became standoffish, and I quickly learned where she drew the line concerning crime: cheating the government was okay; stealing pencils was not okay.

I said earlier that I lowered my expectations of Ed as well as the relationship in order to make the disappointment more bearable. The less I expected, the easier it was to accept nothing.

This declaration reeks of unpleasant boundary lines—or nonexistent boundary lines, to be exact. And this is why I believe what started out as righteous nagging turned to sin during the end times. Boundaries are healthy and godly. The godly approach would have been to establish boundaries as well as consequences for sinful behavior in the marriage—to expect and insist on a godly marriage as close to perfect as humanly possible.

Yes, with difficulties and struggles. Yes, with differences and disagreements. These are expected. Being molested or covering for a lusting spouse are not expected. And consequences—other than nagging—should have been established immediately.

It is heartbreaking to see this in the light of where I drew the line on sin in a marriage. *Actions* like lust, lying, pornography, or

BROKEN umbrellas

neglect in the marriage did not send me across the line. *Words that I was unloved and being treated like a prostitute did.* Actions speak louder than words. They really do. I know that now. However, I was not equipped to think past how those marital deaths hurt me and realize how they hurt God.
I am equipped now, and I give God the glory.

Adam and Eve's sin is a biblical example of setting boundaries and the consequences for breaking those boundaries:

Boundary:
The Lord God placed the man in the Garden of Eden to tend and watch over it. But the Lord God warned him, "You may freely eat the fruit of every tree in the garden—except the tree of the knowledge of good and evil. If you eat its fruit, you are sure to die" (Genesis 2:15-17).

Crossing the line:
So she took some of the fruit and ate it. Then she gave some to her husband, who was with her, and he ate it, too (Genesis 3:6).

Consequences:
Then he said to the woman, "I will sharpen the pain of your pregnancy, and in pain you will give birth. And you will desire to control your husband, but he will rule over you." And to the man he said, "Since you listened to your wife and ate from the tree whose fruit I commanded you not to eat, the ground is cursed because of you. All your life you will struggle to scratch a living from it. It will grow thorns and thistles for you, though you will eat of its grains. By the sweat of your brow will you have

food to eat until you return to the ground from which you were made. For you were made from dust, and to dust you will return" (Genesis 3:16-19).

So the Lord God banished them from the Garden of Eden (Genesis 3:23).

There is no greater example of discovering where someone's line is than the story of Pharaoh within the pages of Exodus.

We are told Pharaoh enslaved the Israelites, and God appointed Moses to lead His people out of that slavery. Moses and Aaron spoke to Pharaoh and delivered God's message that he was to "let God's people go."

Pharaoh refused.

God used Moses to perform a miracle for Pharaoh, and still he wouldn't release God's people. Ten plagues followed—and not random plagues either. Each plague defied one of the gods the Egyptians worshipped.

God sent Moses to turn Pharaoh's river into blood. But because Pharaoh's magicians also turned water into blood, Pharaoh's heart remained hard and he refused to let the Israelites go.

Even after plagues of frogs, gnats, and flies, Pharaoh didn't budge. God released a plague against Pharaoh's livestock, a plague of festering boils over his people and animals, and a plague of hail that ruined Egypt. The hail struck down everything—people, animals, plants, as well as destroyed the trees. Neither a plague of locusts nor a plague of darkness forced Pharaoh to release God's people.

Only after God struck down Egypt's firstborn—including

BROKEN umbrellas

Pharaoh's firstborn—did Pharaoh release the Israelites. This was Pharaoh's line. And yet, even after he gave God's people their freedom, he chased them...until God destroyed Pharaoh and his armies.

Discovering our limits, setting godly boundaries, refusing to cross the line, it's all a process as we grow in the Lord. God knows what it will take to bring us to our knees. He knows where we draw our lines, and they are not always appropriate. We are a work in progress, and God wants our lines to be His lines. While it's good to let hindsight teach us, we can't dwell there or it cripples us. We must move on from our past and into our future, taking growth and wisdom with us. God's boundaries for us fall in pleasant places. And there is nothing more pleasant than being in God's will.

twenty-five

new

name

BROKEN umbrellas

You will be given a new name by the Lord's own mouth (Isaiah 62:2).

String cheese.

Strange way to start a chapter, but I am bound and determined that Satan's name will not start a chapter titled "New Name." So, pass the string cheese and let's get started.

Satan delights in naming us, and the more middle names he can give us, the more he delights! For example, before entering the cave of fasting—and definitely before finding Christ—my name was *Emma Ashamed Unknown Coward Unworthy Lost Bitter Unloved Defeated Broch Stuart.*

I couldn't even fit all that on the application to renew my passport. But it did appear on the name badge of my life for everyone to see. In spite of me gluing my tower of brokenness so I *appeared* healthy and thriving, people knew. Glimpses of my full name showed up in conversations, actions, reactions, parenting, friendships, and my marriage.

And if you think they don't show up in your interactions, you are deceived. Add that to my list of middle names, because I was most certainly deceived into thinking no one knew how broken I was.

When God starts peeling back layers of heart decay, you realize just how many names Satan had assigned to you.

I had a good idea there were a few. During the final years of my marriage to Ed, I occasionally broke free from the oppression and sat in God's presence where He would show me one of Satan's names for me, and then the new name He had waiting for me. Going back into the oppression was so painful after glimpsing the freedom a new name could bring. But only when I allowed God to break that vicious cycle of pain and bondage could He start renaming me.

As you might remember from the funeral, Courageous was my first new name. It replaced Coward, and the cowardly behavior I displayed by trying to hide behind Ed's decision to divorce.

BROKEN umbrellas

Sometimes when children are born, they inherit a name on their birth certificate and don't even realize they have it until they are much older. It is usually a family name passed down that is rarely spoken aloud. Unless the child hears a voice calling them by that name, they don't associate the name as belonging to them.

Satan not only names us, he calls us by that name over and over until we believe it deep in our souls. So much so, that hearing God's new name is foreign to us. Yes, it's on our godly birth certificates, but unless we have heard it spoken to us, we can't associate it as belonging to us.

Bringing me into the cave of fasting was God's way of training me to hear His voice, and only His voice, when He called me by name. There were times I looked around, wondering who He was speaking to because the name was so foreign to me. God's patience never runs out. His love is unfailing, never tiring. I began to see why He needed thirteen months of my undivided attention.

I received a new name during that glorious retreat where God blessed me with not one, but two confirmations. He annihilated one of the names Satan had stamped on me.

The speaker passed out pieces of paper for each woman to write a name Satan had issued to them. By this point in my relationship fast, I knew I had many. But I felt led to write just one: ASHAMED.

The speaker led us to Daniel and spoke of the new name he had been issued. King Nebuchadnezzar attacked Jerusalem, taking captives to Babylon. Daniel was among those captives. The king wanted them trained for serving in the palace, and they were given new names. The king's chief of staff renamed Daniel a Babylonian name—Belteshazzar. These captives in training were given daily rations of food, including meat and wine, from the palace kitchens.

Daniel refused the king's rations—they were unacceptable

to him as an Israelite—choosing instead to eat vegetables and water. God sustained Daniel on this diet, and Daniel went on to be appointed ruler over the whole province of Babylon.

There is so much depth to the book of Daniel, and I encourage you to read about him. For this chapter, I only wanted to show that he was renamed, and he chose to honor God by not accepting the unacceptable. The world tries to impose names on us. Only the names God calls us are worthy of listening to.

John 10:3 says that the Good Shepherd calls His sheep by name. We follow Him because we know His voice. We only know His voice by training our ears to hear His voice.

As the retreat progressed, each teaching session drew us closer to healing and hearing God's new name replace the one we wrote down. God engraved the name UNASHAMED on my heart, soul, and mind. Only intense healing and believing who I am in Christ—and clinging to that—brought me to the place of victory over Satan's most oppressive name for me.

> *The Lord God helps me, so I will not be ashamed. I will be determined, and I know I will not be disgraced* (Isaiah 50:7 NCV).

And Satan stomped and kicked and roared and fought. He insisted, persisted, sent ungodly people to remind me of my shame, and then, like I said before…I rose up. This—Ashamed—was the most harmful name he had appointed me, and God annihilated it.

He's waiting to annihilate your counterfeit names as well. And He has others He's working on in my life. Here are some names God calls you. Start with this list, and add others as He speaks to your heart:

- Masterpiece: "For we are God's masterpiece. He

BROKEN umbrellas

has created us anew in Christ Jesus, so we can do the good things he planned for us long ago" (Ephesians 2:10).

- Treasure: "For you are a holy people, who belong to the Lord your God. Of all the people on earth, the Lord your God has chosen you to be his own special treasure" (Deuteronomy 7:6).
- Beloved: "Beloved, let us love one another, for love is from God, and whoever loves has been born of God and knows God. Anyone who does not love does not know God, because God is love" (1 John 4:7-8 ESV).
- Friend: "I no longer call you slaves, because a master doesn't confide in his slaves. Now you are my friends, since I have told you everything the Father told me" (John 15:15).
- Child: "But to all who believed him and accepted him, he gave the right to become children of God" (John 1:12).
- Heir: "And since we are his children, we are his heirs. In fact, together with Christ we are heirs of God's glory. But if we are to share his glory, we must also share his suffering" (Romans 8:17).
- Son or Daughter: "And I will be your Father, and you will be my sons and daughters, says the Lord Almighty" (2 Corinthians 6:18).

And most importantly:

- His: "But now, O Jacob, listen to the Lord who created you. O Israel, the one who formed you says, 'Do not be afraid, for I have ransomed you. I have called you by name; you are mine'" (Isaiah 43:1).

Emma Broch Stuart

With each healing I receive from an area of brokenness, God gives me a new name. I still can't fit it all on the application when renewing my passport. But it will fit here on the pages of this book.

His Beloved Emma Courageous Unashamed Victorious Known Gentle Found Worthy Loved Daughter of the King Broch Stuart

twenty-six

shamelessly

summarized

BROKEN umbrellas

Woman of God; woman of grace.
Shamelessly I stand, seeking His face.

Harvest comes to a humble heart.
The sun rises; new beginnings start.

Love heals when everything else rages.
Christ's sacrifice paid for sin wages.

New name written down in glory.
Pages fill with my healing story.

The more God renames me, the more I thirst for those new names. I leap ahead, forgetting that it's a journey and I am moving along at God's pace—and I'm not finished until I cross through heaven's gate. I pray you find the courage to let Him work at His pace within your life. It's so much sweeter when He decides, controls, guides, and heals.

As a side note to the New Name chapter, I wanted to share something profound that I came across while in the cave of fasting. *SMITH Magazine* founded a concept called "Six-Word Memoirs" that challenges people to write a short story using only six words.[15]

A friend challenged me to write my memoir in six words. This challenge came after God healed me of past shame and branded UNASHAMED on me, His Beloved. While I am a very wordy, chatty kind of person, I was successful in narrowing my memoir down to six words.

Modern day Samaritan woman stands shameless.

It shows where I've been and it shows where I am now—shameless. Six words express a healing that only God could have orchestrated. It reveals that I have come to terms with a past full of broken relationships. And it radiates a posture of victory in the word *stands*.

Precious friends have given me permission to share their six-word memoirs with you. I pray they touch you as much as they have touched me:

- *Ashes to Life. Risen in Grace.*
- *Always eating words, knowing love wins.*
- *Thought I was alone, but NO!*
- *Never give up, look up there.*
- *1955 memories. I'm reflections of Mom.*

BROKEN umbrellas

- *I will. Pick me, pick me!*
- *Giving up the lead. Letting God.*
- *Dwelling, waiting, expectant amidst hope eternal.*
- *First Born. Ruggedly Handsome. Clean Underwear.*
- *God wins in the end—YAY!*

If we summarized *Broken Umbrellas* in six words:

- *My umbrella is broken. God's isn't.*
- *Wobbling towers. Elephants stampeding. Dust flying.*
- *I married. I died. I grieved.*
- *Children hurting. Ed withdrawing. God enduring.*
- *I am not perfect. Jesus is.*
- *Enough is enough. God has spoken.*
- *I broke. I cried. God rebuilt.*
- *People hurt me, Jesus healed me.*
- *Drowned in shame. Saved by grace.*
- *I was lost, now I'm found.*
- *Neon lights are flashing, "This Way!"*
- *Cave of fasting. God's healing lasting.*
- *Brokenness claimed me. God renamed me.*

If we summarized God and the Bible in six words:

- *God created. We sinned. Jesus saved.*
- *God inspired. People wrote His Word.*
- *Christ broke bread. Symbolized His body.*
- *It rained. Noah floated. Started anew.*
- *Jonah ran. Fish swallowed. Prophet obeyed.*
- *Esther saved her people from death.*
- *Judas betrayed. Christ washed his feet.*
- *Israelites enslaved. Moses led. God delivered.*
- *Jesus bore sins. We live eternally.*

- *Shepherd boy slayed giant, became king.*
- *Ruth gleaned. Boaz redeemed. Naomi rejoiced.*
- *God is love. We are loved.*
- *Guard your heart above all else.*

And now I challenge you to write your six-word memoir. I find it very healing to write one about the past, one about the present, and one about the future. Or write one now and another one in six months. God does some of His best work "in between."

Thank you for sunsets and sunrises.
And the moonlight in between.
Thank you for rainy days, flower gardens, and
for the color green.

Thank you for fresh starts and growing hearts.
And nurturing love in between.
Thank you for calm rest, a comforting embrace,
and humble gifts unseen.[16]

twenty-
seven

rabid

snares

BROKEN umbrellas

In a forest I stand, listening intently to Christ's every word. He speaks; I observe. His hands motion here, gesture there, and whatever He speaks appears right before my eyes when He says the words. His hands never stop moving as He teaches me something important.

On a hill I sit, a valley spread below. Christ converses with me and points out things that are already in place instead of appearing the moment He speaks of them. Fields of grass stretch before the eye; birds fly across the sky.[17]

Just as important as knowing who you are is knowing who you are not. This area of healing was one of the hardest for me because believing something about myself made the truth appear as lies.

This is also one area that God still works on to this day. And I'm here to tell you it does get easier to believe the truth as more and more deep-seated lies and deceit are revealed for what they are—weapons Satan uses to claim your soul.

I trust God to remind me—sometimes daily—who I am and who I am not. Read this chapter as if God is speaking these truths to *you* (because He is!)—even if you don't yet believe them. There is something extremely intimate, powerful, and humbling when we tell God what He already knows. "Hey, God, I am not surrendered to Your truths, but I want to be." God can use that and do beautiful things with it.

Let's make an "I am not" list (that I have personally struggled with) and then we'll spend some time covering each one.

- I am not defined by my past mistakes.
- I am not bound for hell.
- I am not of this world.
- I am not ashamed.
- I am not unworthy.
- I am not defeated.

I Am Not Defined by my Past Mistakes

Satan desperately wants you to believe that you are so he can continue to hold you down in bondage. Let God have your past. He will make something beautiful out of it—like build the foundation of a glorious temple fit for a King.

If anyone acknowledges that Jesus is the Son of

BROKEN umbrellas

*God, **God lives in them** and they in God* (1 John 4:15 NIV, emphasis added).

Just when you start to release your past into God's capable hands, Satan will use anything to try and heap your past back on you. He uses well-meaning individuals, enemies, family, and friends—even yourself. Stand firm in the truth. You are not defined by your past mistakes.

I participated in a restore course that dealt with past brokenness from shame, anger, bitterness, loss. The participants took pieces of paper and wrote down their brokenness, areas of bondage, hurts, and past mistakes. We then took turns entering a room where a wooden cross had been placed. A box of nails and a hammer sat beside the cross and we nailed each piece of paper to the cross. It was the most healing exercise I have ever done, to physically nail my past to that cross.

Nail your past to the cross. And keep nailing it until it stays. That means taking it back to the cross every time Satan deceives you into picking it up again. Taking it back to the cross and nailing it every time Satan says you can't escape your past.

I am not defined by my past mistakes; I am defined as a new creation by Christ living in me.

> *Now we look inside, and what we see is that anyone united with the Messiah gets a fresh start, is created new. The old life is gone; a new life burgeons [blossoms]! Look at it! All this comes from the God who settled the relationship between us and him, and then called us to settle our relationships with each other. God put the world square with himself through the Messiah, giving the world a fresh start by offering forgiveness of sins* (2 Corinthians 5:17-19 The Message).

Believe this truth even when Satan whispers in your ear that it can't be possible, that you have made too many mistakes. God's mercy comes in unlimited supply. When you get off track, let God guide you back. Listen for His voice; it can reach your heart in the form of godly advice from a friend, through the pages of His Word, by a song on the radio, or just that gut feeling you can't explain medically.

Lamentations 3:23 says, "Great is his faithfulness; his mercies begin afresh each morning."

Cling to God's promise. It will start a revolution in your soul. God is faithful, trustworthy, patient, and His mercies are for you. Claim them.

I Am Not Bound for Hell

Truth or lie: "There is no way God can forgive me, I've messed up too badly. I'm bound for hell."

Lie. A big fat deceiving lie straight from the pits of hell and thrown on you like a rabid dog. Grab the Truth Stick and beat that dog.

Sin is not measured by little white sins and big murderous sins, making mine forgivable and yours not. Sin is sin and Jesus died for them all. God doesn't work on a point system in which you reached your limit long ago. Grace is a glorious thing, and it covers *every* thing.

> *But if we are living in the light, as God is in the light, then we have fellowship with each other, and the blood of Jesus, his Son, cleanses us from all sin* (1 John 1:7).

All sin is covered by the blood Jesus freely shed when He

BROKEN umbrellas

laid down His life for us on the cross. When this truth soaked into the broken cracks of my heart, I knelt before the cross with my hands cupped, catching every precious drop of blood that was shed for me. When God healed me from believing this lie, Christ's sacrifice was no longer done in vain.

There was no point in Christ dying for my sins if I continued carrying them instead of leaving them on the cross. This by no means is permission to continue in sin, knowing Jesus bore it all. It should humble us to turn over every area of our life to Him so He can heal us and we can stop carrying sin that Jesus already carried—and died for.

Nail it to the cross. I'm still nailing lies to the cross. And I will continue until I reach heaven. It has nothing to do with little faith/big faith and everything to do with the journey.

Let this truth soak into the broken cracks of your heart. There are many ways God can give you a down-right drenching. Find a local Bible study—or buy a Bible study—surround yourself with godly people who uplift you and sit with you in your pit. God knows what you need; prepare your heart to receive it. And don't dismiss a smile from a stranger or a fluttering bird. God's ways are not our ways (Isaiah 55:8).

I am not bound for hell; I am bound for heaven.

> *But our citizenship is in heaven. And we eagerly await a Savior from there, the Lord Jesus Christ, who, by the power that enables him to bring everything under his control, will transform our lowly bodies so that they will be like his glorious body* (Philippians 3:20-21 NIV).

Head knowledge tells us this truth, but there's nothing like experiencing that saving grace from bondage. It sets us on the right path, puts the Truth Stick in our hand, and allows us to defeat Satan's rabid snares that hold us captive.

I Am Not of This World

When we believe we are defined by past mistakes, and we're held in bondage and the belief we are bound for hell, then we feel there's no hope for eternal life and Satan deceives us into embracing the world as our home. And we are less sensitive to the sins around us, making us more likely to sin. When we replace harmful beliefs with saving truths, we clearly see the separation. We can live for Christ *in* this world without being *of* this world.

> *Do not conform to the pattern of this world, but be transformed by the renewing of your mind. Then you will be able to test and approve what God's will is—his good, pleasing and perfect will* (Romans 12:2 NIV).

> *Do not love this world nor the things it offers you, for when you love the world, you do not have the love of the Father in you* (1 John 2:15).

We are to set ourselves apart from the world without making ourselves unapproachable by the world. There is a balance to achieve, and only God can orchestrate such a balance.

Dave Burchett, in his book *When Bad Christians Happen to Good People*, talks about the sinful world and how much Christians should separate themselves from it. He likens it to fishing without going to the waters where fish are found. He does warn that when we go to the fish, they can be in waters that are polluted.[18]

BROKEN umbrellas

I am not of this world; I am about my Father's business.

In Luke chapter 2, Mary and Joseph misplace Jesus. If you have ever lost a child while shopping, you can surely relate to the panic they must have felt. When they found Him, He was in the temple courts sitting with the teachers, listening and asking them questions. Of course His parents confronted Him. This is what He said to them:

> *"Why did you seek Me? Did you not know that I must be about My Father's business?"* (Luke 2:49 NKJV).

Being about our Father's business allows us to be *in* this world without being *of* this world. That is only possible when being about our Father's business is a lifestyle of obedience, not a Sunday morning activity.

I Am Not Ashamed

The previous two chapters already covered this, but it's so profound that it deserves attention in this chapter too. Shame is a strong weapon in Satan's arsenal—a stronghold that affects many people. I would venture to say it's one of Satan's favorite tactics for imprisoning people within their past.

> *Work hard so you can present yourself to God and receive his approval. Be a good worker, one who does not need to be ashamed and who correctly explains the word of truth* (2 Timothy 2:15).

Let's start by defining *shame*. *Shame* is the leftover residue Satan shoves down our throats after we repent for a sin—and are forgiven. Shame tells us we are wrong. Instead of repenting and basking in Christ's forgiveness, we carry shame and unworthiness around like a concrete block. If and when we mess up again (repent and are forgiven)—yet hold on to the shame—Satan adds another concrete block to our load. You can see where lugging this around saps us of all our energy and takes our focus off God. When our focus is off God, we can't hear His voice calling, "Give it to Me and leave it with Me! You. Are. Forgiven."

> *If we confess our sins, he is faithful and just to forgive us our sins and to cleanse us from all unrighteousness* (1 John 1:9 ESV).

Being cleansed from all unrighteousness means *all* unrighteousness. Therefore, when we continue to pack shame around like a dead horse, Satan does the happy dance. He succeeds in keeping us from an intimate relationship with God.

I am not ashamed; I am shameless.

> *Therefore, since we are surrounded by so great a cloud of witnesses, let us also lay aside every weight, and sin which clings so closely, and let us run with endurance the race that is set before us, looking to Jesus, the founder and perfecter of our faith, who for the joy that was set before him endured the cross,* **despising the shame,** *and is seated at the right hand of the throne of God* (Hebrews 12:1-2 ESV, emphasis added).

Jesus despises shame. We need to recognize it and give it to Jesus (remember, it's a journey)—because He died for it. To hang on to it makes His death a mockery. Feeling guilt is not the same

BROKEN umbrellas

as carrying shame. Guilt says, "I did something wrong." Shame says, "I am wrong."[19] We want to feel guilt—as long as it results in us taking it to the cross and repenting.

I Am Not Unworthy

Our value is often buried under piles of brokenness that have been shoveled on us by others. But we allowed it—and it is up to us to reclaim that value. Dr. Gary Smalley, in his book *The DNA of Relationships* explains that inside each of us, we possess something valuable and worthy and it is susceptible to being harmed or belittled.

> *Whenever you let someone have access to the most sensitive part of you and they start getting careless, you must take back that part of yourself and think,* Excuse me. Apparently, you've lost track of how valuable…I am. But I haven't, and I can't let that happen.[20]

The very fact that God gave His only Son as a ransom for us proves our worth in His eyes. And when we allow others to be careless with our value, we ourselves are being careless.

Jesus Himself told us not to place our value—worth—in the hands of others who will trample it.

> "Don't waste what is holy on people who are unholy. Don't throw your pearls to pigs! They will trample the pearls, then turn and attack you" (Matthew 7:6).

This passage spoke volumes about the value I perceived in myself during the end of my marriage to Ed. God re-established the value of my perceived value. Satan still whispers in my ear that I am worthless—unworthy—and not fit for God's kingdom. God stands up for me; I stand up for me.

I am not unworthy; I am valued.

> "What is the price of two sparrows—one copper coin? But not a single sparrow can fall to the ground without your Father knowing it. And the very hairs on your head are all numbered. So don't be afraid; **you are more valuable to God** than a whole flock of sparrows" (Matthew 10:29-31, emphasis added).

I Am Not Defeated

Deflated, belittled, crushed, conquered, thwarted—God wipes these from our vocabulary and replaces them. Allow Him to change your deflated to inflated. Belittled to approved. Crushed to constructed. Conquered to conqueror. Thwarted to triumphant.

We are at war. It might not be a blood and guts war, but there is a war waging for our souls. God doesn't leave us defenseless; He supplies the weapons we need for battle. Godly weapons—the only kind that will stand up to Satan's weapons.

> *Put on all of God's armor so that you will be able to stand firm against all strategies of the devil. For we are not fighting against flesh-and-blood enemies, but against evil rulers and authorities of the unseen world, against mighty powers in this dark world, and against evil spirits in the heavenly places. Therefore, put on every piece of*

BROKEN umbrellas

God's armor so you will be able to resist the enemy in the time of evil. Then after the battle you will still be standing firm. Stand your ground, putting on the belt of truth and the body armor of God's righteousness. For shoes, put on the peace that comes from the Good News so that you will be fully prepared. In addition to all of these, hold up the shield of faith to stop the fiery arrows of the devil. Put on salvation as your helmet, and take the sword of the Spirit, which is the word of God. Pray in the Spirit at all times and on every occasion. Stay alert and be persistent in your prayers for all believers everywhere (Ephesians 6:11-18).

The belt of truth doesn't come in pieces to pick and choose from, tying just the pieces I prefer into a belt and leaving the other truth pieces on the ground. *All* truth is my weapon. Remember, Satan gives just enough truth to make us believe it's the whole truth. Maybe you have believed—or are believing—other lies about who you are that I haven't mentioned. We must release all lies and replace them with God's truths. Only then can we be completely free.

When we recognize an area of our life that needs healing, Satan is more than willing to leave us alone in this particular area while doubling his forces in another area. It makes us feel like replacing lies with truth is easy. We find ourselves asking, "So why is this other lie so hard to let go of?" Oh, it must be truth.

Wrong.

The Bible says Satan disguises himself as an angel of light (2 Corinthians 11:14). It's a safe assumption that his snares are disguises too.

Jesus said to the people who believed in him, "You are truly my disciples if you remain faithful to my

> teachings. *And you will know the truth, and **the truth will set you free**"* (John 8:31-32, emphasis added).

I am not defeated; I am victorious.

> *But thank God! He gives us victory over sin and death through our Lord Jesus Christ* (1 Corinthians 15:57).

> *I can do all things through Christ, because he gives me strength* (Philippians 4:13 NCV).

> *And because you belong to him, the power of the life-giving Spirit has freed you from the power of sin that leads to death* (Romans 8:2).

Jesus is the key to victory over the lies Satan uses to chain us in bondage. And the path to walking in freedom is a journey. Maybe God is calling you into a cave of fasting where He can have your undivided attention to work through the lies holding you in bondage. He had to be radical with me. Maybe He has to be radical with you.

Or maybe not.

God knows what it will take to break the chains. Trust Him in all things. Bring all lies (darkness) into the Light. The Light gives us truth (Ephesians 5:9). Pray without ceasing. Even reciting one of the psalms to the Creator is holy communication. God's very words created the universe. Study His Word and let Him create beauty from your ashes.

twenty-eight
wicked
dance

BROKEN umbrellas

Depending on how much you've tied your insecurities to men, some of you may have taken a decisive step forward...by recognizing that your vision is badly distorted.... If you look up *at Jesus before you look* out *at men, He will joyfully restore your sight.* [21]

*At one poi*nt during my fast, I tried to break up a fight on the street between two young men, and I got hit in the face. Nothing serious, just a swollen lip. Serves me right, charging in like a bull, thinking I could help. I so desperately wanted the bigger guy to stop hurting the smaller guy. Mothering. I tried to help; nothing worked until a shopkeeper came to the rescue. A sense of relief flooded me when a man arrived on the scene.

Men. I love them. I think. They can be beautiful and godly and offer tremendous comfort and protection when I look past the ones who have hurt me so much.

One of the mistakes I repeatedly made in past relationships was being drawn to men who "needed" mothering. There's this deep satisfaction that comes with nurturing someone and thinking you can make them healthy. It allows you to shove your brokenness down deep, hoping by nurturing someone else you will find healing. It's an unhealthy approach, and over time it will make your brokenness decay even more.

We can't drink dirty water believing it will miraculously turn clean on the way down. It will contaminate every cell in our body. Neither can we cling to a dead vine and pray it gives us life. The hardest thing to accept is that we ourselves cannot nurture someone back to health. Only God can.

Many people have been seriously hurt during their childhood—physically, spiritually, mentally, emotionally, sexually—and those hurts can carry over into adulthood and adult relationships. Satan will stop at nothing to be sure those hurts carry over because then he can feed misconceptions and twist truths—which always ensures more people get hurt.

What a wicked dance to partner a hurting "needy" person with a hurting "need to nurture" person.

Hurting people hurt people.

Over and over and over again.

The most glorious and healthy thing we can do is refuse to let

BROKEN umbrellas

our brokenness hurt other people. Seek healing first, allowing the Healer time to do what only He can do. Then and only then contribute to a healthy relationship.

I know many unhealthy people are already in unhealthy relationships. One of the most beautiful things about God is that He meets us right where we are. He just needs us to be willing to accept whatever it takes to bring healing.

Several men tried to breach the boundaries of my relationship fast. I immediately recognized unhealthy people, and I did not pursue further contact with them. One was doing a similar ministry to one I was involved in, and we exchanged phone numbers. He texted me for personal issues, not ministry issues, telling me more than once that his "morale was in his socks."

I praised God for the opportunity to recognize a hurting needy person. I thanked Him for the chance to push my loneliness aside and hold out for the bigger reward—obediently finishing the "race" He placed before me. I directed this hurting man to God, the only One who could pull his morale out of his socks.

This opportunity showed me how far God had brought me through the healing process. It was so fantastic to realize that God creates space for us to exercise what He teaches us. Encourages us to keep learning through opportunities to be patient, be wise, be transparent…and in my case, be a woman who says no.

An encounter I had during my time of fasting is begging to be retold. This happened at the beginning, while still blinded by past hurts and, in general, bitter toward men. It showed me that when we have been wounded, we tend to gravitate toward those who will wound us in the same ways because that's what we're used to. It's almost like we unconsciously crave being wounded because that's what is familiar to us.

I was standing at the door to my church one evening, when a friend's husband came in and walked right by me as if I wasn't even there. I was so hurt that I made a scene by forcing him to say hello to me. It was ungodly of me because bitterness fueled it, not a pure desire to greet him or be greeted by him. I was out for blood, desiring to prove all men were bad. *See? Told you.*

The next day, I was walking to the school to pick up my daughter. A man in the neighborhood, whom I had seen countless times but never spoken to, was bent over, putting a car seat in his car as I passed him. He stood up, turned his whole body toward me, took a step, and said hello. I was lost in thought and didn't realize he was speaking to me. He repeated his greeting, a big smile plastered across his face. I finally figured out he was speaking to me and returned his greeting.

God knocked me upside the head with my own bitterness. I immediately repented. Can you imagine that poor man after this encounter? We'd never spoken before this. I'm sure he stood there long after I passed by, shaking his head and asking himself, *What just happened?* He had no way of knowing God just used him to teach me a valuable lesson about how I project my bitterness and hurt onto other people.

I had so much unlearning to do.

I'm a little speechless right now as I reflect on who I was then compared to who I am now. I'll be forever grateful to God for revealing who I am. Not that lost soul who had changed in order to adapt to abuse, to make the relationship more manageable and less disappointing. Not that bitter woman who let her past define her.

For change and healing to occur, we must take the first step, which is deciding we won't stay where we are. Always remember that the wicked dance continues until we decide to stop dancing.

twenty-nine

elevator,

eyebrows,

and

men of God

BROKEN umbrellas

Drench a woman in Christ's healing love and she becomes a force to be reckoned with. Before, she was a woman; after, she is a woman after God's own heart.

It's raining right now as I start this chapter that anchors many relational healings from my time in the cave of fasting. I love the rain. Such a glorious gift from above—from the one who waters my soul like He waters the earth.

Men of God were stationed along my journey of fasting from relationships, and relating to them has brought about a healing like no other. There really are godly men in this world; before, I had been too blinded by my own brokenness to even notice. These men of God taught me so much by their example. I watched them love their families with a fire kindled from a deep desire to be all they were created by God to be.

More importantly, I witnessed a devotion to God in them that surpassed any earthly relationship. Even now, these men carry the aroma of Christ everywhere they go as they live out their faith (2 Corinthians 2:14-15). I have been so blessed to be in their cross breeze on many occasions.

I hope they are reading and I hope they know who they are, though I doubt their humble spirits will allow them to be anything but embarrassed by their sister in Christ loving on them so fiercely.

We've just got to talk about these fellas—these awesome creatures of God. Not only have they confirmed me many times along the way, they have prayed with me and over me. They have counseled me and offered so much encouragement. God sent these safe men, my brothers, to minister to me at just the right moment, showering me with so much wisdom and insight.

I even let one of these godly men shave my head. I know, what a crazy way to spring that on you, right? Yup, I shaved my head for a friend who had cancer. I spent several weeks praying about it beforehand, wanting it to glorify God and not be just a meaningless act. I shared this with a brother and he offered to pray for me, and then offered to shave my head if I indeed felt led to do so. What a precious time that was, watching my hair fall

BROKEN umbrellas

to the floor, this man's wife taking pictures to forever remember the moment I went bald. I show those pictures to everyone and we have a chuckle at how big my eyebrows instantly grew.

New brothers in Christ came into my life during my relationship fast and gave me thought-provoking nuggets about God and earthly relationships. Conversing with them within the confines of my relationship fast erased "people pleasing" tendencies, and I crossed the threshold of ending my fast with beautiful friends whom I greatly respect. And they have no idea how their words of inspiration and encouragement soothed my battered heart. Words laid upon their hearts to pass on to me. Wishing me well and hoping that "I feel loved by those who know me." Showing me that sometimes God allows us to start over with a "new vase." Reminding me that I am a princess and the crown I wear is divine, yet worn with humility.

Little by little, I saw all these men of God for the men they are and without any trace of my hurtful past experiences hindering my sight. I saw them as partners, the other half of a God-created team. God made men and women to do kingdom work hand in hand, often partnering in marriage, other times in ministry—sometimes in both. Deep-rooted respect and understanding replaced long-held beliefs that men were abusers, manipulators, self-centered neglectors, cheaters, and life-sapping leeches.

It is greatly disturbing that even with these long-held beliefs, I had still entered relationship after broken relationship. I never stopped seeking and hoping for…I guess I didn't know at the time what I was seeking and hoping for. I was created for relationship and my heart had been longing for that, despite all the brokenness.

I now know my heart was yearning for relationship with Christ, and I sought that in an earthly way, hoping to find healing and a safe space in which to do what I was created for—relate. This established a "seeking a savior" type relationship right from the start, doomed without the Savior.

And to make it even more twisted, I myself had fallen into a "savior" role in those relationships. Talk about a couple of drowning people trying to save each other, each one of us clinging to our past relational baggage that was only pulling us under. There is no way to be saved without letting go of the baggage as well as letting go of the other person, and allowing God to save each of us. It requires a step of faith that He will hold our head out of the water and get us safely to shore.

In my case, Ed and I did not make it safely to shore together. I can only pray there are others standing on the shore, shouting out to him to let go and cling to God.

In John chapter 21, after Jesus's resurrection, He stood on the shore and shouted to His disciples out in a boat. They had fished all night without catching anything. Jesus told them to cast their net on the other side. More fish than they could haul into the boat flopped around in their net. Peter jumped in the water and swam to shore. When the others arrived with the boat and their catch, they found a campfire burning with fish and bread for breakfast.

They settled in around that fire, and three times Jesus asked Peter if he loved Him. Three times—the same number of times Peter had denied knowing Christ. I could just weep at the healing grace Jesus poured over Peter. That redeeming love that soothes, saves, and somehow makes us desire to be better—to be healed.

Those early months around the fire in the cave of fasting were the hardest. One day, I even found myself longing to lay my head on a stranger's shoulder in an elevator. This man had the kindest face and had to squeeze close to me to allow other people inside. He was the perfect height and my head would have fit perfectly against him. It made me cry when I got off the elevator, and I questioned God's strategies concerning this fast.

Gradually, it got easier. Over and over, God took my

BROKEN umbrellas

loneliness—or shame and bitterness—and poured healing grace over me. This sustenance strengthened my desire to be better equipped for relationships. My desire to be healed kept me faithful and obedient. I observed and healed and grew from within the safety of the cave, and actually became a little apprehensive as my fast neared its end.

But as my shelter—my relationship with God—took shape one sturdy board at a time in those early months, it strengthened and has remained steadfast beyond the ending of my fast. Today I'm a different kind of woman. Today I am in a safe place.

thirty

emotion

or

verb

BROKEN umbrellas

Love can be a choice. Love needs to be a choice. Passion makes it easy to pledge one's heart and believe that will be enough to last forever. But the fire of first love is not its proof—its mettle cannot be known until it has passed through the furnace of trial.[22]

During my time in the cave of fasting, God sharpened my senses to marriages around me. One time in church, a brother in Christ prayed aloud, and my heart was instantly seized with an urgency to pray for him and his wife—for their marriage.

During a retreat (following that blessed one full of treasures from God's own hand) I served on the prayer team. We collected prayer cards from the women and then divided them up amongst the prayer group. I still have one of those prayer cards, where a woman wrote a few simple words asking for prayer for her marriage. My heart again was seized and I felt her pain and brokenness.

I don't know who this woman is. But God knows, and there are many like her. Let's take a moment to pray together, you and I:

Father of broken hearts,

We come to You now for this precious wife who filled out that prayer card. She had no idea it would fall into the hands of a divorced prayer warrior who has spent time in that pit. Who understands her marital deaths. Please come into her brokenness and do Your mighty work in her soul. Restore her to complete heart health. I pray this also for her husband, and that individually You draw them so close to You that they feel Your breath upon their cheeks. And then please surround their marriage and bring healing. We pray this for her and for others, in Jesus's name. Amen.

That marriage seminar Ed and I went to is periodically hosted at one church or another in the community. While single, divorced, lonely, and fasting from relationships, I volunteered to help another single woman organize this seminar. My heart

BROKEN umbrellas

ached something fierce as I started decorating tables. Those pieces of me that died during the seminar I attended with Ed came alive to haunt and pierce me again and again.

This other single woman is much older and my relationship with her is so precious. Cultural differences set us up for verbal exchanges that are indeed comical. My favorite is when I hugged her one day and told her I loved her. Her response was, "And you should continue." Actually, culture has nothing to do with it; she's just spunky that way.

It did not escape either of us that we were there, two single women, serving marriages. I was humbly honored that God would give me such a blessing as to partner with her in this way. We prayed over that room of tables and over the couples who would be attending. We added the finishing touches to the decorations. We gave them our all, from the depths of our singleness.

God, in His redeeming grace, took those pieces of me that died long ago and healed them. I still left that church lonely—and I wonder if she did too. But nothing like the lonely I carried out of the marriage seminar that Ed and I attended.

Serving this marriage seminar is a perfect example of God breaking me where I was broken. He entered that wound and gave me the extraordinary opportunity to serve.

And I was safe.

The first time, being a participant, Ed crushed my safety with his lust.

The second time, God redeemed what had been taken from me.

There are many marriages in the Bible worth mentioning. I'd like to take a peek at a few of my favorites.

Abigail and Nabal stand out to me because I can relate to the structure of their relationship. First Samuel 25 tells us Nabal was a wealthy man, but he was foolish. David was traveling through the area with his men and they helped tend Nabal's sheep. David asked for compensation, as was customary. Nabal refused and insulted David, so David told his men to "put on their swords." A messenger approached Abigail and told her what her husband had done.

She immediately took action, gathering food and riding out to intercept David, interceding for the household of Nabal to keep disaster from raining down on them. When she reached David, she jumped off her donkey and bowed before him. Her wise words touched this mighty warrior and are worth quoting here:

> She fell at his feet and said, "I accept all blame in this matter, my lord. Please listen to what I have to say. I know Nabal is a wicked and ill-tempered man; please don't pay any attention to him. He is a fool, just as his name suggests. But I never even saw the young men you sent. Now, my lord, as surely as the Lord lives and you yourself live, since the Lord has kept you from murdering and taking vengeance into your own hands, let all your enemies and those who try to harm you be as cursed as Nabal is. And here is a present that I, your servant, have brought to you and your young men. Please forgive me if I have offended you in any way. The Lord will surely reward you with a lasting dynasty, for you are fighting the Lord's battles. And you have not done wrong throughout your entire life. Even when you are chased by those who seek to kill you, your life is safe in the care of the Lord your God, secure in his treasure pouch!

BROKEN umbrellas

But the lives of your enemies will disappear like stones shot from a sling! When the Lord has done all he promised and has made you leader of Israel, don't let this be a blemish on your record. Then your conscience won't have to bear the staggering burden of needless bloodshed and vengeance. And when the Lord has done these great things for you, please remember me, your servant!" (1 Samuel 25:24-31).

Abigail was a wife like no other, and Nabal took her for granted. Yet, her swift action, humble words, and wisdom saved his household. David accepted her gift and sent her home in peace.

A few days later, the Lord struck Nabal, "and he died" (1 Samuel 25:38).

When David learned of Nabal's death, he sent for Abigail, and "she became his wife" (1 Samuel 25:42).

Priscilla and Aquila were a dynamic team for God. It was customary in that day to identify the husband before the wife, but passages about this couple show Priscilla identified first an equal number of times as Aquila.

Aquila...with his wife Priscilla (Acts 18:2 NKJV).

Aquila and Priscilla greet you heartily in the Lord, with the church that is in their house (1 Corinthians 16:19 NKJV).

When Aquila and Priscilla heard him, they took him aside and explained to him the way of God more accurately (Acts 18:26 NKJV).

[Paul] *sailed for Syria, and Priscilla and Aquila were with him* (Acts 18:18 NKJV).

Greet Priscilla and Aquila, my fellow workers in Christ Jesus (Romans 16:3 NKJV).

Give my greetings to Priscilla and Aquila and those living in the household of Onesiphorus (2 Timothy 4:19).

This husband and wife team truly grasped God's intent for man and woman. Priscilla obviously had many outstanding gifts that allotted her respect and therefore the honor of being identified before her husband on three occasions. What a radical way to confirm a woman of God in her role for kingdom work, by breaking with tradition and bestowing godly honor upon her.

This couple partnered not only in marriage, but in ministry. Besides supporting Paul's ministry, they opened their home and received God's people, and it became a place of worship and teaching.

Aquila and Priscilla's example of God's intent for marriage truly blesses me—neither was made more important than the other. They were equal partners with a common goal: to glorify God.

And finally, I want to mention one more marriage, that of a woman I spoke to years ago. She told me she did not fall in love with her husband until years after being married, after "doing life" with him. When I asked why she married him in the first place, she said their life plans blended perfectly, they were compatible, and it was a match made in heaven.

This baffled as well as impressed me. Love as a verb—action—

BROKEN umbrellas

instead of love as just a noun—emotion.

Sit with me in that for a moment. Because, I don't know about you, but I need to let that soak in. Love is a verb and doing life with someone who shares the same passion of doing life together creates space for love to grow.

It puts a whole new spin on things if you consider love a verb when yoking yourself to another person. How do we take a step of faith and trust that the other also grasps the meaning of love the verb? How do we, as single people, bridge those final few inches and step out in trust? How do we, as married people who have suffered marital deaths, bridge those *miles* and re-trust?

Take a step of faith toward God. He is trustworthy, so I would venture to bet we could practice love the verb (doing life together) on Him first.

> *You must love the Lord your God with all your heart, all your soul, all your strength, and all your mind. And, Love your neighbor as yourself* (Luke 10:27).

God is Love. Not just the creator of it as an emotion as well as a verb, but Love itself—*agape* love. *Agape* gives love even when love is not returned. We can't truly give love the verb to another person until we have first experienced it for ourselves—until we know it deep down in our bones and it becomes the very air we breathe.

> *Love is patient and kind. Love is not jealous or boastful or proud or rude. It does not demand its own way. It is not irritable, and it keeps no record of being wronged. It does not rejoice about injustice but rejoices whenever the truth wins out. Love never gives up, never loses faith, is always hopeful, and endures through every circumstance....* **But**

*love will last forever!... When I was a child, I spoke and thought and reasoned as a child. But when I grew up, I put away childish things. Now we see things imperfectly, like puzzling reflections in a mirror, but then we will see everything with perfect clarity. All that I know now is partial and incomplete, but then I will know everything completely, just as **God now knows me completely**.*

Three things will last forever—faith, hope, and love—and the greatest of these is love (1 Corinthians 13:4-13, emphasis added).

God is waiting with His umbrella to *show* us love the verb. Because God is love itself, we could rewrite 1 Corinthians 13:4-13 and replace the word *love* with *God*. "God is patient and kind. God is not jealous or boastful or proud or rude. God never gives up, never loses faith, is always hopeful, and endures through every circumstance. Three things will last forever—faith, hope, and God—and the greatest of these is God."

Love created this world. Love created us. From that moment to this, love continues to reign, despite humanity's attempts to make it complicated, disposable, or unnecessary.

thirty-one

redeeming

fields

BROKEN umbrellas

To glean in the fields of a godly woman's heart is to glean directly from the Farmer.

I've said it before, and I'll say it again: Arriving is a glorious feeling. My "man fast"—as a friend calls it—is finished. I find myself sitting at the opening of the cave, soaking in sunset after glorious sunset. I now have healthy offerings to contribute to a relationship. I discern new standards in myself, and the ability to accept nothing less. I aim right at the heart, settle there, observe…ponder.

And wait.

I find myself waiting on the Lord. Actively waiting in prayer and delight. Joy and peace fill my waiting hours—my waiting moments. For in this waiting, the Lord continues to pour His sweetness into my life. I want nothing but what He desires for me. To Him be all the honor and glory for now—in this waiting—and forever more.

I don't know what the future holds for me. Only God does. Maybe I will better glorify Him single than partnered with an earthly man. This *must* be my focus, my center, my all: glorifying God above all else. I find immense comfort in this.

During the school of ministry, one of the professors offered an optional workshop one afternoon. In this workshop, we meditated on God's Word. It was the most comforting meditation I've ever experienced. The professor read Psalm 23 several times. She said that whatever valley we are in, God leads. We sin because of fear. She asked us to listen for key words while she read:

> *The Lord is my shepherd; I shall not want. He makes me lie down in green pastures. He leads me beside still waters. He restores my soul. He leads me in paths of righteousness for his name's sake. Even though I walk through the valley of the shadow of death, I will fear no evil, for you are with me; your rod and your staff, they comfort*

BROKEN umbrellas

me. You prepare a table before me in the presence of my enemies; you anoint my head with oil; my cup overflows. Surely goodness and mercy shall follow me all the days of my life, and I shall dwell in the house of the Lord forever (Psalm 23 ESV).

The word "lead" stood out to me the first time. When she read it a second time, I pictured God leading me beside still waters. He was with me in the green pastures; therefore, I trustingly allow Him to lead me through the valley. Because the valley is sandwiched between the pastures and still waters and the prepared table and overflowing cup, it completes the circle and my cup runs over. I am anointed and fed. I feel deep comfort. The path leads straight to waters and pastures, through the valley and to the table. While in the valley, I feared only when I tried to peek around God and see ahead.

After the meditation, the professor asked us how God seemed. My answer: God seemed trustworthy.

We sin because of fear. In this beautiful imagery God gave me, I only feared when I tried to look around Him as He led me.

When He leads my life and I follow, it's more difficult to fall into Satan's sinful snares. When I relinquish all control and allow His will to be done, peace fills me.

Therefore, I am perfectly content to sit in His presence and wait for the future He has in store for me.

No "man fast" is worth its weight in gold without gaining an understanding of what a godly man looks like. Fasting from relationships gave me plenty of time to study God's Word and what He has to say about godly men.

Just as Joseph is one of my favorite people in the Bible, Boaz is right up there too. Did you notice that I gave him a spot in the six-word summaries of the Bible? Here it is again:

Ruth gleaned. Boaz redeemed. Naomi rejoiced.

That sums up the book of Ruth, though my summary lacks depth. If we get out of the "romantic story" mindset, we see that depth. Let me give you a little backstory.

Naomi and her husband, along with their two sons, moved to Moab because there was a famine in Bethlehem. Once there, Naomi's husband died and her two sons married Moabite women. Then her two sons died, leaving Naomi with two daughters-in-law. Ruth was married to Naomi's son Mahlon. Naomi decided to return to her people, and Ruth insisted on going with her. "Wherever you go, I will go; wherever you live, I will live. Your people will be my people, and your God will be my God" (Ruth 1:16).

It's important to note that Ruth and Mahlon were married for ten years and no children are mentioned. It's also important to know that the Moabites worshiped the god Chemosh and therefore practiced human sacrifices—which all of my research shows included children.

Upon returning to Bethlehem, Ruth gleaned in fields in order to provide for her mother-in-law. "As it happened" (Ruth 2:3) she gleaned in a field belonging to Boaz. I just love that "as it happened." I've told you before, I don't believe in coincidence. As it happened indeed!

Boaz was one of Naomi's kinsman-redeemers. Coincidence? I think not. (Goodness, I love this story!) Boaz came to the field and noticed Ruth. Not that she was foreign, but he noticed her character. He was told that she came with Naomi from Moab. She worked in the field steadily except for a short break to rest.

He approached her and encouraged her to stay in his field through the harvest, gleaning with his servant girls, and he offered her water whenever she was thirsty. His favor surprised Ruth, and she asked him why he had taken notice of her, a

BROKEN umbrellas

foreigner who had no entitlement to any of these things. Boaz's answer is so precious. He confirms her character—all she had done for her mother-in-law and leaving her people.

At mealtime, Boaz made sure Ruth had something to eat. When Ruth returned to Naomi after gleaning that day, Naomi asked her whose field she had worked in. Ruth's simple answer holds so much depth: "The man I *worked with* today is named Boaz" (Ruth 2:19, emphasis added). *Worked with*. Ruth worked with Boaz. I see God's plan already taking shape. Partnered. And united in kingdom work.

It might be hard to understand Naomi's intentions when she then sent Ruth to the threshing floor in order to "woo" Boaz. I believe Naomi was in constant communication with God, pleading on their behalf, and praying for intervention in their situation. Sending Ruth in her best clothes to the threshing floor was Naomi giving God space to reveal His will for their lives.

Kelly Minter, in her Bible study *Ruth: Loss, Love & Legacy* from "The Living Room Series," says this about Ruth's garments: "When we're wrapped in garments of mourning, we're unavailable for whatever else God has for us.... Though we can't be certain what Ruth had on, we know her new dress signaled a change, a readiness, an availability to Boaz and to God for the possibility of something new."[23]

It's a safe bet that Ruth had remained in mourning after losing her husband, making her off limits. Her courage to change and go to Boaz is astounding. And I can't miss that she had to have thought she was barren since no children are mentioned to have resulted from her union with Mahlon.

Boaz revealed that there was a kinsman-redeemer above him, but Boaz spoke to that kinsman-redeemer and discovered he wasn't interested in redeeming Naomi's husband's land because it meant inheriting a Moabitess widow.

Ruth and Boaz married, and verse 13 of Ruth chapter 4 says that God enabled Ruth to conceive. Makes you wonder why during those ten years in Moab God hadn't enabled Ruth to conceive. Could the evil practice of child sacrificing have anything to do with it? Perhaps God was saying, "Not yet. Hold out for the bigger prize. You are meant for kingdom purposes."

Boaz and Ruth's son was also meant for kingdom purposes—a place in the genealogy of Christ.

I encourage you to read about Ruth, really dig in and get to know this godly woman—and the godly man who redeemed her without even knowing his decision would lead to the birth of the world's Savior.

Boaz is a standard by which all godly men could be measured. Whether you are divorced and healing, single and seeking, or already married to your Boaz, I pray you find contentment with the future God has for you.

thirty-two

above

all

else

BROKEN umbrellas

"Now listen, daughter, don't miss a word: forget your country, put your home behind you. Be here—the king is wild for you. Since he's your lord, adore him. Wedding gifts pour in from Tyre; rich guests shower you with presents." (Her wedding dress is dazzling, lined with gold by the weavers; all her dresses and robes are woven with gold. She is led to the king.) ~ Royal Wedding Psalm (Psalm 45:10-14 The Message)

I can't think of a better place to talk about wedding vows than right here, following chapters on marriage and Boaz... after sharing so much of my journey that led and continues to lead to God and His commitment to me (and mine to Him).

I must admit, I dislike traditional wedding vows. They aren't even biblical. Traditional wedding vows were written by religious folks for the Church of England's *Book of Common Prayer* in 1662. It just gets my goat that the Royal Wedding Psalm wasn't considered, or passages from the book of Song of Solomon.

These glorious sections of Scripture are Spirit-filled. The Message is a translation of the Bible that's a little less conservative. I chose it as the opening to this chapter because of the part about the king being wild for his bride. Can you imagine attending a wedding and hearing the bride and groom exchange vows about being wild for each other? It would be all I could do not to jump up and whoop and holler.

I, Boaz, take thee, Ruth, and vow to be wild for you.

Talk about wild.

Solomon wrote some of the most beautiful poetry in the Bible. I am not equipped to offer you anything other than my opinion and share some of my favorite passages. I'll leave the deep theology to more mature theologians.

Within the seven poems of Song of Solomon, we have three "speakers." The Beloved (bride), the Lover (Solomon), and friends. In Song of Solomon chapter 1 verse 4, the friends say, "We rejoice and delight in you; we will praise your love more than wine" (NIV).

Because God laid the marriages of my precious friends on my heart, this passage truly blesses me. We have to be healed individuals to rejoice and praise a couple's love without letting jealousy or bitterness stab at us.

And if during a wedding, the bride and groom's friends stood up and recited vows taken directly from God's Word, it would

BROKEN umbrellas

indeed be a celebration.
We, friends of the bride and groom, vow to rejoice and praise their love more than wine.

I like to think of the friends in Song of Solomon as this couple's own personal cheerleading squad. Or rope holders. I believe it blesses God when we invest in marriages other than our own.

The imagery within the pages of Song of Solomon tantalizes the senses. To compare the wedding bedroom to a forest, the bed to lush foliage, and the groom to a young stag. To compare lips to scarlet ribbon, breasts to fawns, and hair to tapestry. To be called radiant, beautiful one, majestic. And no one has ever complimented my sandaled feet.

One more favorite passage:

> *Awake, north wind! Rise up, south wind! Blow on my garden and spread its fragrance all around. Come into your garden, my love; taste its finest fruits* (Song of Solomon 4:16).

Though we're tempted to blush, let's keep in mind this is Scripture. God's Word is alive and powerful (Hebrews 4:12). So much beauty in these few words. I would most certainly whoop and holler if I heard these recited as vows. Beloved refers to herself as a garden, then gives ownership of her garden to her groom (Lover), and invites him to taste her garden's finest fruits. Glorious! Those fruits are most certainly fruits that strengthen their relationship. Fruits that encourage each of them to grow and mature. Fruits like joy and kindness. Beloved is offering her groom to taste her joy, taste her kindness—her character.

> *But the Holy Spirit produces this kind of fruit in our lives: love, joy, peace, patience, kindness,*

goodness, faithfulness, gentleness, and self-control (Galatians 5:22-23).

Is anyone else bothered by the phrase "lawfully wedded wife/husband" in traditional wedding vows? I pledge for this chapter that we change it to "God-fully wedded wife/husband."

I, Ruth, take thee, Boaz, to be my God-fully wedded husband.
I, Boaz, take thee, Ruth, to be my God-fully wedded wife.

Even better than that would be:

I, Ruth, take thee, Boaz, and vow to be your wedded wife full of God.
I, Boaz, take thee, Ruth, and vow to be your wedded husband full of God.

Let's spend this chapter rewriting wedding vows. We can go back to the traditional ones tomorrow, but for today, what would your wedding vows say?

- I, Ruth, take thee Boaz, and vow to partner with you for kingdom work.
  Two people are better than one, because they get more done by working together. If one falls down, the other can help him up (Ecclesiastes 4:9-10 NCV).

- I, Boaz, take thee Ruth, and vow to try and resolve arguments before the sun goes down.
  Don't let the sun go down while you are still angry

BROKEN umbrellas

(Ephesians 4:26).

- I, Ruth, take thee Boaz, and vow to be your helper.
  Then the Lord God said, "It is not good for the man to be alone. I will make a helper [ezer] who is just right for him" (Genesis 2:18).

- I, Boaz, take thee Ruth, and vow to pray for you.
  Pray for each other (James 5:16).

- I, Ruth, take thee, Boaz, and vow to rebuke and then forgive.
  "If another believer sins, rebuke that person; then if there is repentance, forgive. Even if that person wrongs you seven times a day and each time turns again and asks forgiveness, you must forgive" (Luke 17:3-4).

- I, Boaz, take thee, Ruth, and vow to put God above you.
  "Seek the Kingdom of God above all else, and live righteously, and he will give you everything you need" (Matthew 6:33).

The Bible offers so much relational richness. We could scour passages and come up with thousands of godly vows. Vows to disappoint or hurt—because we are human—and vows to repent. Vows to lose our way, and then seek God's will. Vows to stumble and fall, yet get right back up again. Vows to succumb to selfishness, bitterness, anger, shame, and then take our brokenness to the cross. And vows to seek forgiveness.

From Genesis to Revelation, God is reciting vows (promises) to us, the Church—His bride. I imagine standing before the world, face-to-face with Him, my vows echoing in response to His. My sobs carry on the wind because I know I'll never fulfill every vow. I know I will stumble. I will fail Him. He reaches over, tenderly places His hand over my heart, and says, "This is the voice I listen to above all else."

thirty-three

knee to knee

BROKEN umbrellas

Restlessness. Wandering hearts that need to feel the breeze blow from a different direction, carrying new scents and stirring new passions.

Nothing solidifies growth and healing like being drawn into a season of *being* instead of *doing*. *Doing* helped me believe I had value. I served in many areas with a women's ministry—the same ministry that organized those retreats and Bible studies that became some of God's tools for healing my brokenness. I wore nearly a dozen hats, and loved every one of them. They stretched my hospitality and organizational skills while at the same time providing a safe place for spiritual growth and healing to my soul.

But then God decided I was finished serving under these hats. It was time to stand firm in my healing without anything holding me up but Him. I went through an entirely different kind of pain when my hands weren't "busy" for Him. How God brought me out of one season and into the other is part of my journey and therefore belongs here, among the ending chapters of *Broken Umbrellas*.

I was very content, serving and doing for God. There wasn't any task I backed away from, and I did this serving without the luxury of a car, using public transportation instead. I even carried spaghetti sauce in my backpack across the city—by bus and tram—in order to serve twenty people.

I'm not trying to toot my own horn; I only want to show how committed I was to serving God's kingdom. My heart, grateful heart at how far the Father had brought me, gushed forth and I couldn't do enough. God did teach me how to say no to certain things, but that only made serving in other areas stronger.

God and I were in perfect harmony, zigging here and zagging there. Can I do that? Sure I can. Can I do this? Of course. Will I go there? You bet.

And then I said yes one too many times. God immediately convicted my heart and spoke these words, "You did not seek My will on this." I had said yes to a huge commitment, and I repented for not going to the Lord first. I asked Him to take it from me—send someone to replace me—if He indeed did not

BROKEN umbrellas

want me fulfilling this commitment. He did not take it from me, instead He let me fulfill my commitment.

But He made sure I remembered what being out of His will felt like. I suffered migraines while doing this particular ministry—no matter how good and fulfilling this ministry was, it wasn't one God had planned for me. My guts twisted while serving in this area, and only in this area. My soul was heavy.

God thoroughly and utterly disciplined me. The Bible says in Hebrews 12:5-6: "My child, don't make light of the Lord's discipline, and don't give up when he corrects you. For the Lord disciplines those he loves, and he punishes each one he accepts as his child."

He had my attention and indeed sent a breeze blowing from a different direction. He no longer wanted me "doing." But He knew my root value was integrity, and my definition of integrity was to be a promise keeper. He graciously allowed me to ease into this new season by finishing well the commitments I was already under.

When God was convicting me, and sending a breeze to blow from a different direction, I believed He only wanted me to "trim" my areas of serving. I started by not renewing any commitments. Then I finished serving in other areas, and resigned from them as well. But there were two commitments I desperately clung to, the two areas of serving that I loved doing more than anything. I begged God not to take them from me.

While I was struggling with this, an amazing ministry team from South Africa came to my church and ministered to us through prayer and several workshops. It was during a prophetic art workshop that God spoke to my heart and I was able to release these last two ministries. Opening my hand, I allowed God to take them. I don't want to reveal the details of this workshop, in case any of you ever get the chance to participate in a prophetic art class. I urge you to say yes if anyone asks you to attend because the blessings I received are so beautiful. I still draw on that experience when seeking God's will.

Was it coincidence that at the very moment I clung to something God didn't want me clinging to, this ministry team just happened to be at my church? I don't think so. God always amazes me at the things He uses to bring me closer to Him.

I found myself twiddling my thumbs with nothing to do for God. What now? I imagined myself in a white room with two chairs. God sat in one, I sat in the other. We were knee to knee. He spoke. *"Who are you?"*

"You know who I am, Lord."

"Who are you?"

I looked around for something I could serve—do—and found nothing. I bit my nails.

He drew me back. *"Who are you?"*

I searched that ivory room for something to divert my attention and again found nothing—except Him.

He took my hands and asked again, *"Who are you?"*

What could I say? A control freak extraordinaire? A mess? A wallflower? I could always *show* Him that I am a snorting sobber—literally. Many answers ran through my head, but I knew that any answer with the word "a" before it would not suffice.

I then aligned my gaze with His. "I am Yours."

A smile radiated from Him. *"Who are you?"*

"I am Yours."

"Do you believe it?"

I nodded. "I am Yours."

"Who are you?"

"I am Yours."

"Do you believe it?"

"I AM YOURS!"

"You are Mine."

"I AM YOURS!"

BROKEN umbrellas

"You are Mine."

This is what God and I did during my season of being. Repeated over and over that I am His, and not because of any ministry I "did." Not because of serving or being His hands and feet.

I sat with nothing to offer but my heart. I sat expecting nothing. And still He gave. Trust in Him strengthened. Faith grew. Joy overflowed. I snuggled in the safety of Him. I sat at His feet and soaked in His presence. Those breezes blowing from new directions carried new scents and stirred new passions.

Now here I am, in a season of writing with a message that more than anything, God wants you to know *you* are His, and if you aren't, you can be.

thirty-four

baby

wind

BROKEN umbrellas

Heaven is a storehouse of once broken pieces now made eternally whole.

Emma Broch Stuart

When I first arrived at the morgue to see my grandson Alex, I felt an urgency to get his footprint before doing anything else. His daddy and mama were going to need that in the coming months. Oh how I wept while standing over him, putting his tiny foot on the ink pad. I then took several pictures, not sure if they turned out or not because I couldn't see anything through the tears. After, I picked him up and sang to him.

When I got home that evening, I downloaded the pictures and noticed how wet his face looked. I then realized that while standing over him, my tears had fallen on his tiny cheeks and nose. I treasure those photos of his grandma's grief covering him.

Out of all my brokenness, nothing has hurt me quite like witnessing my oldest son's brokenness from losing his baby. It's a helpless brokenness. There was nothing I could do to take that pain from him while at the same time grieving myself. My son doesn't walk with the Lord, but I prayed over him anyway. God gave me the strength to dress my little prince for his funeral, to hold that broken baby body and rock him, sing to him. I read him my favorite children's book and filled his coffin with flower petals.

Sometimes while grieving you have to really look in order to see God's handprint on a situation. How on earth we ended up with duplicate stuffed elephants is beyond me. God knew. This grandma wrapped one of those elephants inside the blanket that held my precious one. The other elephant comforted his mama and daddy.

I choose to celebrate the day my grandson was born, not mourn the day he died—which of course is the same day. On the first anniversary of his birth, I covered his gravesite with helium balloons. What gorgeous colors swayed in that winter wind.

Kelly Minter, in her Bible study *Ruth: Loss, Love & Legacy* from "The Living Room Series," talks about what it means to "weep going forward." She says, "Although there will be weeping in this life, the direction in which we weep is what truly

BROKEN umbrellas

matters."[24] This was in reference to Ruth weeping yet moving forward with Naomi, and Orpah weeping yet moving backward. (She returned to her people.)

Through this broken experience of losing Alex, I clung to one passage in the Bible. Matthew 6:20 says to store your treasures in heaven. My grandbaby is one such treasure, safely tucked within the folds of heaven where nothing can harm him. It is because of that I am able to "weep forward."

I wrote a children's book, titled *The Windkeeper,* about a windkeeper who trains the four winds of heaven for their role in fulfilling God's greatest rescue mission—the birth of His Son. I dedicated the book, "For my son Cameron, your 'baby wind' waits for you in heaven."

Brokenness around us is easier to see than the brokenness within ourselves. But when we deal with our own brokenness, God gives us this incredible ability to sit with others in their brokenness. They still hurt, and we hurt for them.

We were meant to "do life" together in spite of our brokenness. And that is a beautiful thing.

thirty-five

love

notes

BROKEN umbrellas

Arms crossed, I stand with my back against a closed door, pouting. Things aren't going my way. My life has fallen apart and control is no longer mine.

Was it ever mine?

I've closed Him out. After all, He deserves it; it's His fault I'm hurting.

But...I still need Him in some areas of my life, so I only shut the door on painful places in my heart. Places I don't trust Him to carry me through. The suffering is too great.

A piece of paper brushes against my bare foot and I reach down. Little hearts color one side; poems, promises, and words of love cover the other side. Before I finish reading, another sheet of paper touches my foot.

God—Creator of the universe—is slipping me love notes under the door.

During that restore course I mentioned earlier, the speaker, Audrey Jose, asked the group if we'd ever seen pictures of Christ in churches standing at a door and knocking. She said these pictures usually represented Christ standing at the door of a sinner's heart. The book of Revelation was written by the apostle John and this particular section of passage—Revelation 3:20—was written to the Church in Laodicea. It was written to believers, not sinners.

Audrey asked us to imagine our hearts like a house. We keep our stuff (hurts, bitterness, shame, loss) inside rooms with the doors closed. We allow God access to some doors, but not all of them. It's at these doors our Savior stands and knocks.

God gave me this beautiful image of slipping me love notes several years ago while I processed the news that my best friend had cancer. The pain of her diagnosis was so great, I buckled under the pressure of it. The terror that ripped through me at the realization of what she would endure broke me into a million pieces. I slammed that door in God's face, and for a time refused to let Him comfort me. He never left the other side of that door. He not only sent in His troops to minister to me along the way (love notes), He waited for *me* to let Him in. Not once did He chastise me. He let me ask all those hard questions, let me go through the five stages of grief at my own pace.

I grieved a "loss" but not a physical one. My friend is still very much alive and now cancer free. God chose to heal her this side of heaven, though I never asked Him to. The one prayer I cried out over and over for her was that God would protect her heart and her soul. That no matter the brokenness and pain from this trial, she would not turn from Him.

The loss I grieved was the loss of our friendship structure. No longer could she invest in our friendship, and I again learned to give the greatest form of love there is. *Hesed* love. The decision to love when nothing could be given in return. To give completely

BROKEN umbrellas

of myself until I was empty, knowing that God would fill me. God sustained the friendship. I didn't, and neither did my friend. I grew so much during her battle with cancer. We are both different people—stronger people—because of it.

Had my friend's diagnosis come during the darkest time of my life, I'm not sure our friendship would have survived my selfishness and brokenness. God's work in my life is the only reason this story has a glorious ending with two friends stronger from the battle.

thirty-six

joy

boxes

BROKEN umbrellas

Misery hates living alone. Misery seeks companions, and it doesn't discriminate. It rejoices when downtrodden hearts join those in the trenches. Misery deceives you into believing you'll find strength in numbers. The line is drawn, and you stand on that line. Misery screams for you to cross to its side where many wait to feed you from your own wretchedness—recycling the lies you feed yourself. The tiny voice of joy beckons from the other side of the line. Glimpses of a table overflowing with harvest catch your eye, and Joy stands there, waiting to serve you.

Logic tells us that many broken, miserable people joining forces would be stronger than a few joy-filled people refusing to conform to misery's bondage. But this simply is not true. God's logic is not human logic.

God's people giving thanks reaches heaven's ears with joyous song. To train our hearts to focus on the joy instead of the heartache in our lives requires being intentional in giving thanks. The very act of mouthing sincere thanks heals a little part of us. Before we know it, huge clumps of ourselves find wholeness. Before we know it, gratitude becomes a lifestyle, not just a phrase uttered before meals.

Circumstances have a way of hindering our joy, causing mounds of bitterness and despair to override thanks. We reach the point in our walk with Christ where we realize that while we change and circumstances change and feelings change and lives change, God never changes. And there is holy gratitude in that fact.

Gratitude is so much more than a prayer in passing. It becomes ingrained in you to find joy in all things at all times. Gratitude comes from trusting when there is no evidence to even prompt trust. Gratitude comes from knowing who you are, who you are not, and who God is. Gratitude heals. It beats bitterness to a pulp. Gratitude is the outpouring of a thankful heart.

After reading the book *One Thousand Gifts*,[25] I started a gratitude journal. I shared an excerpt with you at the beginning of chapter 4. I'd like to share a bit more. My prayer is that it encourages you to start your own gratitude journal and to find those joy-treasures hidden in every circumstance, carried on every breeze, and waiting to be snatched up by a grateful heart.

> *Splashes of red and purple on desert brown*
> *Barriers, fences, and walls—gates, openings, and doors*
> *Night-time bunny hops across yards*

BROKEN umbrellas

Circumstances...all of them
Vitamin D and how God provides it
Meals I don't have to cook
Cotton fields and that anything worth harvesting is worth the prickly work
When my mama calls me "Dollie"
God's city under snow
The thought of a grandbaby
Coming to the place where all is well no matter what isn't
Smoochie-cheek game
The color green
Sweet sleep where I wake feeling like I've been cradled
Finishing well
Rainy days
How grape leaves grow big and "cover" their fruit while it's growing
The crinkly sounds of Christmas stockings being filled
Trees
Attics
Countdown to something big
Joy boxes, Emmy style
Storms on tin roofs
Lost umbrellas blowing down the highway
Campfires, autumn leaves, lazy kitties
Children's books
Artsy friends and the gifts they bestow upon me
Clocks
Cherry limeades
Real desire to be real and knowing only God can ensure authenticity
Arriving

A precious friend displays random boxes all over her house that she calls "Joy Boxes." Inside, she stores mementos from her life—a little book she made when she was a child, her son's bad report card from years ago, handmade gifts from her children, letters, a painted stone. To open one and peek inside is to witness pure joy. Her personal joy. Our joy cups overflow with God's goodness. We just have to train our eyes to see it. To become a "glass is half full" kind of person. To believe the best in people, circumstances, and ourselves.

Training my eyes has brought a complete transformation in me—to find joy in everything, which simultaneously brings healing. To thank my Creator for every single breath He graciously allows me to breathe. If I want to be a change agent and bring Light into all the world, it must start with me—and it must be authentic. God makes it authentic. He just needs a willing, humble heart that desires healing from brokenness.

Gratitude is what filled that void I mentioned earlier after leaving Ed. It was instrumental in transforming deep-rooted brokenness into deep-rooted gratefulness. Gratitude carried me from *that* place to the place I am now. And it will carry me to my heavenly home where I will spend eternity showing gratitude.

Until then, I will continue to live a lifestyle of thanks giving. Thanks given for the hard things and thanks given for the beauty around me. Thanks for the work God has done in my life and will continue to do until I reach the "end of construction."

And He reminds me when I get off track. Satan will never stop warring for my soul. I catch myself being bothered, or irritable, or unthankful. God prompts my heart in those cases. He desires so greatly that I find each and every thing a gift from His very hand.

Recently, I was complaining to God about a person whose negativity rubbed me the wrong way. God stirred my heart with these words, "I gave this person to you. She is a gift from Me—broken though she may be. She is My gift to you."

BROKEN umbrellas

Gratefulness flooded me. Not only for His "gift," but also that He didn't let me simmer in that ungratefulness. I thanked Him for reprimanding me, for forgiving me, and for putting this person in my life.

Genesis 6:5-6 says, "The Lord observed the extent of human wickedness on the earth, and he saw that everything they thought or imagined was consistently and totally evil. So the Lord was sorry he had ever made them and put them on the earth. It broke his heart. "

Verse six in the New King James Version says, "He was grieved in His heart."

God grieves when we are ungrateful. We all understand this; every one of us has witnessed rude, ungrateful spirits that don't settle well within us. Ungratefulness in my children was the one thing that sent their noses to the corner. I struggle even now not to be rude to cashiers who rush me through their line and don't thank me for my business. Such a small thing, but imagine it on a bigger scale…like giving an entire universe to someone who won't even glance up from their cellphone.

Years ago, I worked for a Christian company that started the day with prayer. We each took turns e-mailing a prayer to the group. It was during a period of time when my transformation from bitterness to gratefulness was brand new and I was nauseatingly chipper. I have since found a balance of living a lifestyle of gratefulness without it patronizing people. Here's the prayer I sent one spring day:

Father,

Bless this awesome, energized, spring-blooming day! Bless those partaking in the beauty that is budding around us. For those who are not partaking in the beauty, may they trip and fall and notice a ladybug or a blossoming flower. I wish I could fly so I could sprinkle happiness and flower petals on everyone! How marvelous are Your creations, and how marvelous that we receive the full harvest of them!

Tripping and falling for You.

My prayer now would be that people embrace the Source of true joy, and God would do whatever it took to bring them to their knees in humble gratefulness. I guess tripping and falling isn't such a bad thing, if that's what it takes to turn someone's grumbling into gratitude.

Here's another prayer that seems appropriate for this chapter:

Lord,

You clothe us in more than physical ways. Long flowing gowns of joy swish around our feet while crowns of sweet memories circle our heads. And how do I even describe the colors! You must look down on us and see a magnificent rainbow. Each thing we do for Your service and glory must paint another colorful stripe across Your heart. Help us be Your rainbow today.
Dress us this morning as You see fit and according to life's weather. If we need boots to trudge through this earthly muck, then please make them sturdy. If our day calls for joyful dancing, then don't forget our tap shoes so we can really make a noise for You while swaying to life's music. I volunteer to be the green stripe in Your rainbow today.

BROKEN umbrellas

Colorfully yours.

If you prepare your joy boxes, I promise God will supply the joy.

thirty-seven imperfect skirts

BROKEN umbrellas

While making cookies with my daughter and her friend, I had the incredible opportunity to speak truth into these young hearts. While sliding the hot cookies from the sheet onto the table, my daughter's friend said she only liked the perfect round ones, not the lopsided, broken ones. My daughter agreed. I said I preferred the ugly, broken ones. Of course they asked why, so I shared with them that lopsided cookies represent life and people—me—more accurately than perfectly round cookies. And I was okay being lopsided and broken and letting Jesus be the perfectly round Cookie.

I am praying over this book as I write it. It hasn't fallen into your hands by coincidence. Maybe you've arrived at this chapter, where God asked me to present the gospel a là Emma style—imperfect and wordy—and you don't have a relationship with Jesus. Maybe you have arrived, know Jesus, but don't know how to present the gospel to someone. I pray God empowers you to take a step of faith by being vulnerable with someone about where God has brought you. It starts there—showing the world why you are so passionate about your first Love.

So, here we go. One imperfect Christian (that would be me) coming right up!

More than likely you have been introduced—exposed—to Christianity at some point in your life. Whether or not that experience had a positive impact on you depends on a couple of things: one, your state of mind and heart; and two, how that exposure was presented.

We are all imperfect humans—including Christians. Imperfect means that we do things imperfectly. We say things imperfectly. Christians sometimes show Christ to the world imperfectly. But it is "eternally" dangerous to use the gospel presented to you imperfectly as your reason for not accepting Christ. God says in His Word that every knee will bow before Him. Every knee.

Every tongue will confess that Jesus is Lord. Every tongue. Now, whether this is done here on earth or in heaven before the Creator, it *is* going to happen. If we wait until we are bowed before Him to confess that He is Lord, it is too late. Our eternity will not be spent in heaven. It will be spent in hell (Revelation 20:15).

Philippians 2:9-11 says, "Therefore, God elevated him to the place of highest honor and gave him the name above all other names, that at the name of Jesus every knee should bow, in heaven and on earth and under the earth, and every tongue

BROKEN umbrellas

declare that Jesus Christ is Lord, to the glory of God the Father."

The blame game will not work with God. You and you alone are responsible for responding to God wooing you to salvation.

Romans 1:20 says,

> *For ever since the world was created, people have seen the earth and sky. Through everything God made, they can clearly see his invisible qualities— his eternal power and divine nature. So **they have no excuse for not knowing God*** (emphasis added).

To me, this means no one can hide behind the imperfect skirts of a Christian. Don't wait for the gospel to come to you. Seek! Seek with all your heart!

> [If] *you seek the Lord your God, you will find him if you seek him with all your heart and with all your soul* (Deuteronomy 4:29 NIV).

Christians *are* called to go into the world and share the Good News of Jesus Christ (the gospel). And Christians are doing that. Christians can be doing *more* of that. But whether or not someone has presented Christ to you, God has given you many opportunities to learn about Him. He gave us His Word—the Bible. There are biblically sound churches on every corner where you can hear the gospel message. Just in my little town of 575, there are 5 churches. Five! And Psalm 19:1 says, "The heavens declare the glory of God; the skies proclaim the work of his hands" (NIV). We can't gaze around at this gorgeous earth that sustains us without knowing that Someone sustains us.

No one can stand before God and say, "I didn't know."

Romans 3:23 says that everyone has sinned and falls short of God's glory. God is in charge. This is His universe, and He says we must keep His commandments. James 2:10 shows us that we'll never keep them on our own because, "For the person who keeps all of the laws except one is as guilty as a person who has broken all of God's laws."

The penalty for breaking His commandments—sin—is death. Romans 6:23 says that the wages of sin is death. We don't have to physically commit murder to be guilty of murder. God says in Matthew 5:21-22, "You're familiar with the command to the ancients, 'Do not murder.' I'm telling you that anyone who is so much as angry with a brother or sister is guilty of murder" (The Message).

"But God showed his great love for us by sending Christ to die for us while we were still sinners" (Romans 5:8).

So, why was Jesus necessary? Because sin entered God's perfectly created world, perfectly created people. God is holy, and He cannot be in the presence of anything unholy. I think about a person inside a germ-free environment. We cannot enter their environment without taking measures—protection—to keep that person from coming in contact with our germs. God would be the person and Jesus would be the protection. I am by no means saying God is sick, I'm saying that just like a cancer patient cannot be in an environment with germs, God cannot be in the presence of sin. Jesus is the bridge between us and God. Therefore, He is very necessary.

"Jesus told him, 'I am the way, the truth, and the life. No one can come to the Father except through me'" (John 14:6).

Let's go back to those imperfect Christians. Many people believe that being a Christian means you have to be perfect, and that can be one excuse they use to deny Christ—they know they'll never be perfect. And they have a past full of examples

BROKEN umbrellas

of that imperfection. But accepting Christ has nothing to do with being perfect—past, present, or future. Christians are not perfect until they reach heaven.

I have seen images of Ruth Bell Graham's gravestone. It reads: "End of Construction. Thank you for your patience."[26] I couldn't have said it better myself. Christianity is a journey. We are being molded into the likeness of Christ on a daily basis.

Christianity is simply surrendering your life to Christ so He can do transforming work in you that brings Him glory. It is believing God sent His Son to die a sinner's death on a cross—though He was sinless. It is believing that Jesus rose from the dead—defeating the grave—and is now in heaven.

Christianity is also coming to the place in your life where you admit you need a Savior. This is also a hiccup for many people. Eternal life is far from their minds because the here and now life is going so well. Or it's going poorly and they blame God.

Just a step deeper than the "fire insurance" of eternal life is that "created for relationship" I've been talking about on the pages of this book. God created people to glorify Him through a relationship with Him. That is our purpose, and we all have the same purpose. How we glorify God can look different for each of us because we are individuals and in different places in our lives. God meets us there, works *with* us and *through* us there.

And after we realize our need for a Savior, believe in all Jesus did for us, we need to confess that need and that belief. Accept the free gift of salvation. "God saved you by his grace when you believed. And you can't take credit for this; it is a gift from God. Salvation is not a reward for the good things we have done, so none of us can boast about it" (Ephesians 2:8-9).

Being transformed is not a journey we take alone. Not only does God supply the Holy Spirit to dwell in us and guide us in truth, He prompts His people to lend a hand. Yes, imperfect broken people, but His people nonetheless.

And the most glorious thing about Christianity is that it is a *personal* relationship with Jesus. Oh, so very personal. It makes me jump with joy because it is so tailored to me and me alone. While the basics are the same for each of us, everything else is truly mine and no one else's. We do have to watch that a spirit of comparison doesn't wiggle its way through the door. There's nothing worse than seeing someone else's relationship with Jesus and feeling that it's stronger than our relationship with Jesus. Or easier, or more beautiful. Jesus is relating to you where you are—where He wants you to be.

One example of this would be to see the life of a missionary as glamorous while you're at home ministering to your five children on a daily basis, or caring for elderly parents. It's all for God.

Find a church and pour your heart out to God, and if you come in contact with the sharp edges of an imperfect Christian, go again. Don't let that experience keep you from your prize. Find a mountaintop—or bow your head right where you are. God is waiting to cover you with His umbrella. You have but to step under.

thirty-eight

go
knowing

BROKEN umbrellas

Ask God to start a revolution in relationships, one relationship at a time, starting with your relationships. Pray that the revolution will spread until people across the world are given the chance to be safely known, graciously explored, hopefully discovered, and powerfully touched.[27]

It took less than a half an hour for three movers from Crown Relocations to pack my treasures for shipping overseas. My daughter and I arrived back in the states before our treasures.

Almost a year has passed since arriving. My daughter is doing better at building new relationships that I am—maybe her youth has something to do with it. I'm often homesick for France where I was "powerfully touched" and where I'm "safely known." God has not yet revealed His reasons for bringing me back to my roots. I may never know, and that's okay. He said *go* so I went, and now I've arrived. Revolution will happen here like it happened there. Everything He brings me to—and brings me through—is for His glory, and besides, I'm safely known by the only One who matters.

God is waiting to powerfully touch you, too. He wants to explore, discover, and delight in you—even more than He already does—as you grow in Him. And you've always been safely known.

Nothing you have endured—or inflicted—can keep you from being healed. Your umbrella may be broken, but God is the Glue that fixes the most hopeless of broken things. Maybe you've pondered leaving a legacy and what that looks like right now, at this moment in your life. God specializes in helping us leave a legacy of healing.

Every document, e-mail, or business card Crown Relocations put into my hand carried their company slogan: Go Knowing.[28] Two words that offer tremendous comfort. Two words that foster growth and healing. Two words that promise solid ground upon which to put two feet. I can think of no better way to close *Broken Umbrellas* than with those two words.

We must first *go* before we can *arrive*. Arriving is a glorious feeling. Taking the first step of going is the hardest. I encourage you to take that step—or a great big flying leap—and revolution will come. It starts with the One Relationship that matters most.

BROKEN umbrellas

Go knowing Who holds the umbrella.
Go knowing Who goes before you.
Go knowing Who goes with you.
Go knowing Who walks beside you.
Go knowing Jesus died for you.
Go knowing you are not alone.
Go knowing you will arrive safely.
Go knowing you will arrive healed.

thank you, danki, merci, grazie

When *thank you* could never express the deepness of a heart brimming with gratitude, I try saying it in foreign languages. But even *merci* fails me now when bubbles of thanks rise to the surface as I write my list of thank yous. There aren't enough foreign languages to truly show how much I appreciate each of you.

To my birthday buddy—who maintains a steady supply of smiles, love, and sound advice—thank you.

Howard, my "walking Bible," thank you for Bible addresses and for knowing what I believe. You were a huge part in molding those beliefs. Wally, my other "Bible with legs," thank you for the single word that totally changed one profound sentence.

Men of God who will remain nameless here, but never in my heart. You are so precious to me.

Thank you, Tammie, for all things girly.

Rope holders, both past and present, how does a once broken soul ever thank you for the countless times you carried me to the King? To Anna, Michelle, Anne, Jenjen, Lilia, Karen, Amy, Terri, Dianne, Jill, Janice, Rene, Diane, Patti, Audrey, Emmy, the one who calls me Dollie, and Kim… thank you.

Sandi Flower gets her own paragraph. Thank you for loving non-fiction…just this once. Thank you for always hearing my heart above all else, no matter what may spew from my mouth. Thank you for building memories with me here on earth and for not beating me to heaven. Thank you for being my Flower.

Gail, how many times have you read *Broken Umbrellas*? Saying thank you in a dozen languages would never express how much I appreciate you and the time you've invested into seeing BU all the way to the very end.

Kristy, thank you for letting me practice on you. Precious heart, you are so loved. Thank you for being transparent, and letting me be the same. And thank you for being a "metaphor-ish" kind of gal who gets me.

Thank you editors, proofers, influencers, endorsers, and readers. It takes a village, it really does. As we walk one another home, may the journey be healing, conversations uplifting, fellowship sweet, and arrival a thing to celebrate.

WhiteFire Publishing guy, David, and gals, Roseanna and Dina, thank you for all you do. You make it look effortless, but I know the behind-the-scenes truth. You are so appreciated. Each of you holds a significant part in making *the Spirit Meet the Page*.

To the One who makes my heart love deep, the Reason gratitude bubbles to the surface, the Voice who calls me Beloved, the Source of true healing, the Builder of life's foundation, the All-knowing, Almighty, Creator of beautiful things, the Song I sing, the Focus of my praise, the Only stable thing in this unstable world, the Peace-whisperer, Hope-giver, and Heart-mender…I adore You.

references

1   Carolyn Custis James, *When Life and Beliefs Collide* (Zondervan, 2001), 19.

2   Beth Moore, *So Long, Insecurity: You've Been a Bad Friend to Us* (Tyndale, 2010), 342.

3   Carolyn Custis James, *The Gospel of Ruth* (Zondervan, 2008), 115.

4   Gary Chapman, *The Five Love Languages: How to Express Heartfelt Commitment to Your Mate* (Northfield Publishing, 1992, 1995, 2004), 60.

5   Ibid., 107.

6   Jarrid Wilson, http://jarridwilson.tumblr.com/post/31360783999/i-heart-jesus-org-let-not-the-opinions-of-man, accessed March 31, 2014.

7   Taken from *It Had to Be a Monday* by Jill Briscoe. Copyright © 1995 by Tyndale House Publishers, Inc. Used by permission of Tyndale House Publishers, Inc. All rights reserved.

8   Larry Crabb, *Soultalk: Speaking with Power into the Lives of Others* (Thomas Nelson, 2003), 91-92.

9   Copyright 2013 Francis Chan. ***Crazy Love: Overwhelmed by a Relentless God*** published by David C Cook. Publisher permission required to reproduce. All rights reserved.

10   Lifesprings School of Ministry, Grenoble, France, 2010-2011, adapted from the WomenSchool of Ministry Leadership founded by Pamela H. Heim, established with Lifesprings School of Ministry's founding president Anna Pavey and led by Janice Gutierrez, Dean and current Executive Director of Lifesprings Women's Ministries International.

11   Taken from *The Gift of Being Yourself* by David G. Benner. Copyright© 2004 by David G. Benner. Used by permission of

InterVarisy Press, P.O. Box 1400, Downers Grove, IL 60515, USA. www.ivpress.com

12   Emma Broch Stuart, *Barn Doors*.

13   Copyright© 1999 by LifeWay Press®. Living Proof Ministries, Inc. Updated 2009. Second printing August 2010. Beth Moore, *Breaking Free: The Journey, The Stories*. Reprinted and used by permission.

14   Vance Havner, *Hearts Afire* (Revell, a division of Baker Publishing Group, 1952).

15   http://www.sixwordmemoirs.com/, accessed August 22, 2014.

16   Emma Broch Stuart, *Barn Doors*.

17   Images I received while participating in Lectio Divina on Matthew 6:25-34.

18   Dave Burchett, *When Bad Christians Happen to Good People* (WaterBrook Press, 2002), 134.

19   Wayne Platt, professor, counselor, and keynote speaker in the UK, "Leadership from the Inside Out; Qualifications, Qualities & Character," Lifesprings School of Ministry, Grenoble, France, 2010.

20   Taken from *The DNA of Relationships* by Dr. Gary Smalley. Copyright © 2004 by Tyndale House Publishers, Inc. Used by permission of Tyndale House Publishers, Inc. All rights reserved.

21   Taken from *So Long, Insecurity: You've Been a Bad Friend to Us* by Beth Moore. Copyright © 2010 by Tyndale House Publishers, Inc. Used by permission of Tyndale House Publishers, Inc. All rights reserved.

22   Adapted from *Jewel of Persia* by Roseanna M. White (WhiteFire Publishing, 2011).

23   Copyright© 2009 by LifeWay Press®. Seventh printing 2012. Kelly Minter, *Ruth: Loss, Love & Legacy* "The Living Room Series." Reprinted and used by permission.

24   Ibid., 22.

25   Ann Voskamp, *One Thousand Gifts* (Zondervan, 2010).
26   http://www.ruthbellgrahammemorial.org/RBG_Obituary.asp, accessed March 9, 2014.
27   Used by permission. *Soultalk: Speaking with Power into the Lives of Others*, Larry Crabb, 2003, Thomas Nelson. Nashville, Tennessee. All rights reserved.
28   https://www.crownrelo.com/intl/en-us/, accessed August 22, 2014.

www.ingramcontent.com/pod-product-compliance
Lightning Source LLC
Chambersburg PA
CBHW070142100426
42743CB00013B/2797